West Y...

Mountain Biking

South Pennine Trails

VERTEBRATE **PUBLISHING**

Design and production by Vertebrate Publishing, Sheffield
www.**v-publishing**.co.uk

West Yorkshire
MountainBiking
South Pennine Trails

Written by
Benjamin Haworth

West Yorkshire
MountainBiking
South Pennine Trails

ISBN 978-1-906148-15-7

Front cover: Jon Woodhouse and Jenny Collett above Todmorden. Photo: Sim Mainey.
Back cover: Tom Fenton in Newsholme Dean. Photo John Coefield.

  All maps reproduced by permission of Ordnance Survey
on behalf of The Controller of Her Majesty's Stationery Office.
© Crown Copyright. 100025218

 Design & production by Nathan Ryder.
www.**v-graphics**.co.uk
Printed in China.

MIX
Paper from
responsible sources
FSC® C010256

Contents

SECTION 1
CALDERDALE BOROUGH

ROUTE GRADES
▲ = MEDIUM ▲ = HARD ▲ = EXTREME (see page ix)

SECTION 2
BRADFORD BOROUGH

SECTION 3
KIRKLEES BOROUGH

SECTION 4
CITY OF LEEDS BOROUGH

Introduction

West Yorkshire is a unique area to ride. The mix of nature and industry, bleak remoteness and accessibility. It contains what the National Office of Statistics call the 'West Yorkshire Urban Area'. This is the 143 square mile conurbation of Leeds, Bradford, Huddersfield and Wakefield that is highly urbanised and populated (1.5 million people) but also incorporates substantial areas of agricultural land within it. And it's incorporated in various beguiling, bizarre and beautiful ways.

Unlike pretty National Parks, West Yorkshire doesn't get overloaded with other outdoor users. Its lack of obvious scenery and lofty peaks means it doesn't appear on a lot of people's radars. West Yorkshire isn't about clambering to the top of a summit and taking in the majestic vistas below you. West Yorkshire is about valleys. Steep sided valleys. West Yorkshire is about trails. Oodles of noodles trails. West Yorkshire is quite clearly made for mountain bikers.

Having said that, it can be beautiful. But the beautiful moments you encounter are modest and surprising, which makes them strangely potent. It's all about juxtaposition. To be frank, you'll pass through some pretty grim places on your way to some pretty amazing places. The routes in this book take you on a journey – mini-adventures – taking in bleak moorland, ugly suburbia, woodland singletrack, quaint rurality, forgotten packhorse trails, motorway bridges, reservoirs and housing estates.

You're not getting away from it all, you're taking it all in.

Geologically speaking most of West Yorkshire is on a massive lump of Carboniferous rock. So you don't encounter the rolling greenery of limestone areas. It may not ever reach particularly high altitude but it makes up for that in gradient. Look at the contour lines on a map of the South Pennines and you will see that it's a mix of broad flattish moorland tops with super-steep slopes falling off the edges into the myriad valleys.

And what about the trails? The riding in West Yorkshire is all about the trails. Sociologically speaking we have history to thank for these. The industrial heritage of the textile industry and the maze of horse-friendly tracks and trails that that industry required and created. A great deal of these routes have avoided being turned into roads as they're just too skinny or precipitous to cobble or tarmac. Other routes have been simply been abandoned in their ancient state as there's no longer any practical reason for people to use them.

So yes, West Yorkshire is full of skinny, precipitous, abandoned impractical paths. What more could any mountain biker want?

Benjamin Haworth

Acknowledgements

Big thanks to those West Yorkshire residents who have guided me around their local trails over the past few years: Dave Anderson, Felix Harris-Evans, Tim Kershaw, Barney Marsh, Clive Nutton, Ed Oxley, Seb Ramsey and Craig Woodhouse. Thanks to Chris Fishlock for being my co-pilot in the early years of exploring and getting lost. Thanks to the people at Singletrack Mountain Bike Magazine for choosing to base their operation in West Yorkshire and affording me ample opportunities to get out and about. Huge thanks to my wife Charlotte for putting up with muddy floors, maps strewn everywhere, late nights, borrowing the car and for being generally an absent husband during the time this book was being assembled.

How to Use This Book

Riding in West Yorkshire

This book breaks West Yorkshire down into the four key boroughs for mountain biking: Bradford, Calderdale, Kirklees and the City Of Leeds.

Believe it or not, the borough of Bradford is actually a rather lovely place. It's pretty. The trails in this borough are about quality not quantity. There's minimal bleak moorland and maximum sheltered singletrack. There are still some steep climbs to deal with but the descents are a bit shallower and as such give great value for money.

Calderdale takes up almost half of this book. There's a good reason for this: it's absolutely chock-full of trails. It's a land of steep sided valleys and stark moortops. Stick to the valley side trails in soggy conditions as the moortops aren't much fun if it's grim.

Kirklees is where you'll find the most remote-feeling riding in West Yorkshire. Most of the routes in this chapter take you across some decent stretches of open countryside. These are gorgeous if the skies are clear and the ground is firm. They're hard work if it's damp and dank. The Mirfield and Dewsbury route is reasonably all-year friendly though.

The riding around the City Of Leeds borough is a real revelation. It doesn't look very promising on the map but threading their way through the suburbs are sections of real mountain biking joy. A lot of the riding is fairly easy-going but the brief pockets of singletrack are intense, technical and extremely rewarding.

The Routes

This guide contains the best routes in West Yorkshire (in our opinion!). The aim is to encourage you to ride new trails in new areas, and to help you get to know the region. Try the routes as suggested, in reverse or joined to neighbouring rides. Once you've ridden a few and got to know what's what, you'll be able to link sections together to create your own rides.

Grades

Routes, climbs and descents are graded blue, red and black, in a similar system to that used at trail centres around the UK.

▲ = Easy   ▲ = Moderate   ▲ = Hard

Blue graded routes are generally shorter routes and are within reach of most MTBers, even newcomers, as well as the kind of thing you could do in a short day or when the weather's really foul. **Reds** are the kind of rides that won't actually take a full day, but you'll probably not want to do anything else once you've ridden them. And **Blacks** are those big and memorable days out that will demand endurance and some technical ability in places. These are the kind of routes to work up to.

The grades are based on average conditions – good weather and not too wet and muddy. In a drought the routes will feel easier, in the depths of winter, harder. Grades consider technicality, length, climbs, navigation, and remoteness – so one 'black' route might be a short all-out technical test while another could be a big endurance challenge with tricky navigation. As ever, these grades are subjective. How you find a particular route, downhill or climb will be dictated by your own levels of fitness and skill.

Directions & Accuracy

While every effort has been made to ensure accuracy within the directions in this guide, things change and we are unable to guarantee that every detail will be correct. Please treat stated distances and times as guidelines. **Please exercise caution if a direction appears at odds with the route on the ground. A comparison between direction and map should see you on the right track.**

Rights of Way

Countryside access in the UK hasn't been particularly kind to cyclists, although things are improving. We have 'right of way' on bridleways (blue arrows on signs) and byways (red arrows). However, having 'right of way' doesn't actually mean having the right of way, just that we're allowed to ride there – so give way to walkers and horse riders. We're also allowed to ride on green lanes and some unclassified roads, although the only way to determine which are legal and which aren't is to check with the local countryside authority. Obviously, cycle routes are also in.

The very understanding Forestry Commission generally allows cyclists to use its land (again, you'll need to check with them first to be sure). You must, however, obey all signs, especially those warning of forestry operations – a fully loaded logging truck will do more than scuff your frame...

Everything else is out of bounds (unless, of course, the landowner says otherwise). Riding illegally can upset walkers (who have every right to enjoy their day) and is, in many cases, technically classed as trespass (meaning you could be prosecuted for any damage caused). Not all tracks are signed, so it's not always obvious whether that great-looking trail you want to follow is an illegal footpath or a legal bridleway. That's why it's a good idea to carry a map with you on every ride.

The Bike

Generally any half-decent mountain bike (try and avoid a '£99 Special') will be fine for riding these trails. For the harder routes, a full-suspension bike could add comfort and control, while a lightweight race bike might make the hills easier.

Check everything's working – especially for harder riding. You won't be going uphill fast if your gears seize but may be quicker than planned if your brakes don't work. Pump the tyres up, check that nothing's about to fall off or wear through and check that everything that should be tight is tight.

Essential Kit

Helmet

"The best helmet is the one that you're wearing". Make sure it fits, you're wearing it correctly and that it won't move in a crash.

Clothing

You need to get your clothing right if you want to stay comfortable on a bike, especially in bad weather. The easiest way to do this is to follow a layering system. Begin with clothing made from 'technical' synthetic or wool fabrics that will wick the sweat away from your body and then dry quickly, keeping you dry and warm. Stay away from cotton – it absorbs moisture and holds onto it. If it's chilly, an insulating layer will keep you warm, and a wind/waterproof layer on the outside protects from the elements. Layers can then be removed or added to suit the conditions. Padded shorts are more comfortable, but the amount of lycra on display is down to you. Baggy shorts, full length tights and trousers are all available to match the conditions. Set off a little on the cold side – you'll soon warm up. Don't leave the warm clothes behind though, as the weather can turn quickly.

Gloves

Gloves ward off blisters and numb hands and help keep your fingers warm. They also provide a surprising amount of protection when you come off.

Footwear

Flat pedals/clips-ins – it's your call. Make sure you can walk in the shoes and that they have sufficient tread for you to do so. Consider overshoes if it's chilly.

Other essentials

As mentioned, take any necessary spares, tools, tube and pump, spare clothes, first aid kit, food and water. Stop short of the kitchen sink, as you'll still want to be able to actually ride your bike.

You'll need something to carry this lot in. We'd suggest a hydration pack, as they allow you to drink on the move and keep excess weight off the bike.

Maps

The rides in this book are covered by four **Ordnance Survey** maps:
Explorer OL21 South Pennines, 1:25,000
Explorer 277 Manchester & Salford 1:25,000
Explorer 288 Bradford & Huddersfield 1:25,000
Explorer 289 Leeds 1:25,000

General Safety

The ability to read a map, navigate in poor visibility and to understand weather warnings is essential. Don't head out in bad weather, unless you're confident and capable of doing so.

Some of the routes described point you at tough climbs and steep descents that can potentially be very dangerous. Too much exuberance on a steep descent in the middle of nowhere and you could be in more than a spot of bother, especially if you're alone. Consider your limitations and relative fragility.

Be self-sufficient. Carry food and water, spares, a tube and a pump. Consider a first-aid kit. Even if it's warm, the weather could turn, so take a wind/waterproof. Think about what could happen on an enforced stop. Pack lights if you could finish in the dark.

If you're riding solo, think about the seriousness of an accident – you might be without help for a very long time. Tell someone where you're going, when you'll be back and tell them once you are back. Take a mobile phone if you have one, but don't expect a signal. And **don't** call out the ambulance because you've grazed your knee.

Riding in a group is safer (ambitious overtaking manoeuvres excepted) and often more fun, but don't leave slower riders too far behind and give them a minute for a breather when they've caught up. Allow extra time for a group ride, as you'll inevitably stop and chat. You might need an extra top if you're standing around for a while. Ride within your ability, make sure you can slow down fast and give way to other users. Bells might be annoying, but they work. If you can't bring yourself to bolt one on, a polite 'excuse me' should be fine. **On hot, sunny days, slap on some Factor 30+ and ALWAYS WEAR YOUR HELMET!**

In the Event of an Accident

In the event of an accident requiring immediate assistance: Dial **999** and ask for **POLICE** or **AMBULANCE**. If you can supply the services with a grid reference of exactly where you are it should help to speed up their response time.

Rules of the (Off) Road

1. Always ride on legal trails.
2. Ride considerately – give way to horses and pedestrians.
3. Don't spook animals.
4. Ride in control – you don't know who's around the next corner.

5. Leave gates as you find them – if you're unsure, shut them.
6. Keep the noise down and don't swear loudly when you fall off in front of walkers.
7. Leave no trace – take home everything you took out.
8. Keep water sources clean – don't take toilet stops near streams.
9. Enjoy the countryside and respect its life and work.

Planning Your Ride

1. Consider the ability/experience of each rider in your group. Check the weather forecast. How much time do you have available? Now choose your route.
2. Study the route description before setting off, and cross-reference it with the relevant map.
3. Bear in mind everything we've suggested about safety, clothing, spares and food and drink.
4. Get out there and get dirty.

Maps & Symbols

Ordnance Survey maps are the most commonly used, are easy to read and many people are happy using them. If you're not familiar with OS maps and are unsure of what the symbols mean, you can download a free map legend from **www.v-outdoor.co.uk**

We've included details of the relevant OS map for each route. To find out more about OS maps or to order maps please visit **www.ordnancesurvey.co.uk**

Here's a guide to the symbols and abbreviations we use on the maps and in our directions:

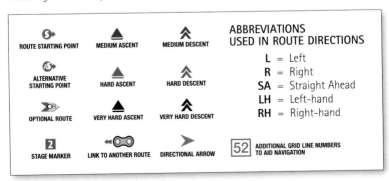

			ABBREVIATIONS USED IN ROUTE DIRECTIONS
ROUTE STARTING POINT	**MEDIUM ASCENT**	**MEDIUM DESCENT**	**L** = Left
ALTERNATIVE STARTING POINT	**HARD ASCENT**	**HARD DESCENT**	**R** = Right
OPTIONAL ROUTE	**VERY HARD ASCENT**	**VERY HARD DESCENT**	**SA** = Straight Ahead
STAGE MARKER	**LINK TO ANOTHER ROUTE**	**DIRECTIONAL ARROW**	**LH** = Left-hand
			RH = Right-hand
			52 ADDITIONAL GRID LINE NUMBERS TO AID NAVIGATION

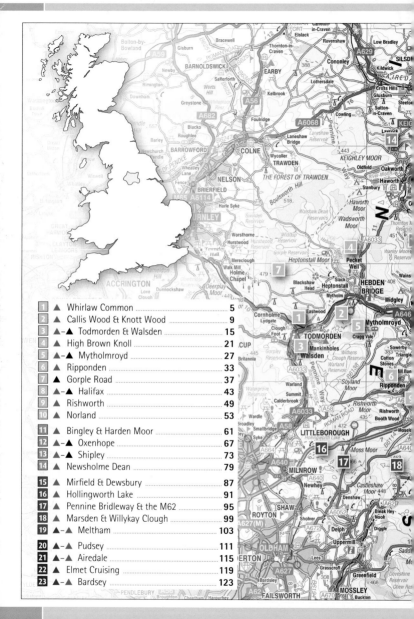

West Yorkshire
MountainBiking
Area Map & Route Finder

SECTION 1

Calderdale Borough

Calderdale has the largest amount of high quality riding of all the boroughs in West Yorkshire. The area is covered with bridleways, byways and broken roads. Packhorse slab tracks, moorland trails, rubbly chutes, slippy singletrack, stupidly steep climbs, scary fast descents, eye-popping scenery, forgotten worlds, unexpected technicality, unpredictability and an impressive all-year round rideability. You can see why some people never ride anywhere else.

LUMB FALLS (ROUTE 04) **PHOTO: BENJAMIN HAWORTH**

HALIFAX HEATHER PHOTO: BENJAMIN HAWORTH

APPROACHING WHIRLAW STONES PHOTO: BENJAMIN HAWORTH

Introduction

Starting at the very handy Rodwell End picnic site situated in between Todmorden and Hebden Bridge this route is a tale of two halves. The first half is about going up. The second half is about going down. A veritable hardy perennial that always delivers the goods.

The Ride

A warm up along the canal towpath takes you into the centre of Todmorden. Then the not-too-busy Burnley road takes you out of town past the recently renovated park (which you can cycle through if you'd rather avoid road riding as much as possible). Then the hard work begins – getting yourself up on to Whirlaw Common. Although the tracks are quite wide, their steepness and unrelenting nature is always a test – they always seem to get steeper and rougher as they near the end as well. Thankfully once you're up, you're up. The rest of the route makes great use of the hills. It includes the area's trademark stone slabbed packhorse trails as you pass below Whirlaw Stones, tight technical trails past the golf course, fast flowing singletrack down to Cross Stone and the final twisty, rocky descent to Rodwell End never fails to raise a grin.

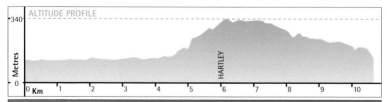

WHIRLAW COMMON   **GRADE:** ▲

TOTAL DISTANCE: 11KM » **TOTAL ASCENT**: 250M » **TIME**: 1.5–2 HOURS » **START/FINISH**: RODWELL END PICNIC
SITE CAR PARK » **START GRID REF**: SD 956247 » **SATNAV**: EASTWOOD » **PARKING**: RODWELL END PICNIC SITE CAR
PARK » **OS MAP**: EXPLORER OL21 » **PUB**: NONE » **CAFÉ**: THE BEAR CAFÉ, TODMORDEN TEL: 07714 333 230

Directions – Whirlaw Common

⑤➤ Turn **R** out of the picnic site car park and follow road for 200m before turning **L** and meeting canal towpath. Turn **R** and follow canal towpath for 2km. Pass under the road via a dark narrow tunnel. Once through the tunnel turn around 180 degrees and get on the road you just passed under. Turn **L** along the road.

2 **R** at roundabout and follow road for 2km into Lydgate. Branch **R** off the main road opposite some industrial units and head up single track road. This road turns sharply right after 150m and becomes rougher. Follow this main track as it snakes its way uphill for 500m to a gate.

3 Go through the gate and climb up the grassy track alongside the fence. After 100m turn **R** away from the fenceline and climb up track for 100m to a gate. Go through the gate and climb up the track past Orchan Rocks for 350m to meet a junction with the Calderdale Way bridleway.

4 Turn **R** and follow the bridleway for 1km. After 1km go through gate and follow stone slab packhorse trail for 200m to a gate. Go through the gate and head downhill passing below Whirlaw Stones on more packhorse trail for 500m.

5 Upon joining a farm road turn **R** and follow double track downhill for 400m. **SA** at track crossroads up a steep, rough, walled climb that levels off after 50m before heading downhill on tight singletrack. After 250m turn sharply **L** up a short awkward walled climb and then descend into golf club car park.

6 **Ride slowly** out of the car park and turn **R** at junction with a road. After 50m turn **L** at the road and follow road for 500m to Bean Hole Head House. Turn **R** after the house down walled bridleway and follow this track for 500m until it ends with a short sharp climb to join a farm track.

7 Turn **R** along farm track, bending **L** after 50m and then after 150m turn **R** and head into farmyard area (watching out for children and animals). Turn **L** in the farmyard and head down walled singletrack that then zigzags you down the hill. Be careful as you enter the picnic site car park at the bottom.

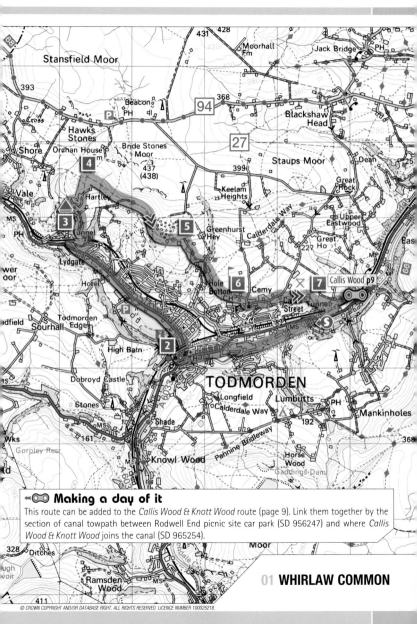

⟜◯◯ Making a day of it

This route can be added to the *Callis Wood & Knott Wood* route (page 9). Link them together by the section of canal towpath between Rodwell End picnic site car park (SD 956247) and where *Callis Wood & Knott Wood* joins the canal (SD 965254).

01 **WHIRLAW COMMON**

Introduction

A lot of this ride is on wide farm roads and minor singletrack roads but it's far from easy or dull. Some of the climbs are incredibly steep in places and of a duration to test anyone's legs. The sections of singletrack are brief but brilliant. This route is an excellent tour of the valley.

The Ride

The start of this route is straight up a stereotypically steep Hebden Bridge singletrack road climb. It's not nice but the benefit is an impressively swift height gain. Once the tarmac is over it's a simple case of following the Pennine Bridleway across the lower flanks below Stoodley Pike. The descent back down to the valley floor isn't as drawn out as the climb but it packs in a couple of spicy sections and is generally excitingly fast for the most part. Getting back out from the valley floor again involves a big climb. Initially tarmac but the latter half is Pennine Bridleway. After a steep chute down into Colden you traverse around to Slack where you hit a great section of skinny fast singletrack. After a sharp climb into the lovely Heptonstall it's downhill all the way back to Hebden Bridge, taking in part of the classic Blue Pig trail and the infamous slippy cobbled Buttress.

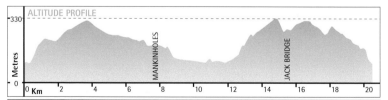

ALTITUDE PROFILE

330

Metres

MANKINHOLES

JACK BRIDGE

0

0 Km   2   4   6   8   10   12   14   16   18   20

CALLIS WOOD & KNOTT WOOD   **GRADE:** ▲

TOTAL DISTANCE: 20.5KM » **TOTAL ASCENT**: 580M » **TIME**: 2–3 HOURS » **START/FINISH**: HEBDEN BRIDGE
START GRID REF: SD 992273 » **SATNAV**: HEBDEN BRIDGE » **PARKING**: HEBDEN BRIDGE » **OS MAP**: EXPLORER OL21
PUB: STUBBING WHARF, HEBDEN BRIDGE, TEL: 01422 844 107 » **CAFÉ**: COFFEE CALI, HEBDEN BRIDGE, TEL: 01422 845 629

PHOTO: JOHN COEFIELD

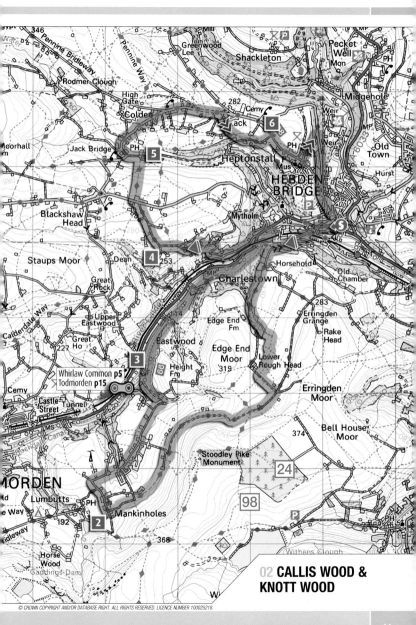

02 **CALLIS WOOD & KNOTT WOOD**

Directions – Callis Wood & Knott Wood

↪ Head out of Hebden Bridge towards Todmorden on the main road. At Co-op Supermarket on your left take the rising road **L** past the car park entrance and over the canal. Turn **R** up Horsehold. Follow this very steep road for approx. 1km. As the now cobbled road bends left, take the signposted gate **SA** on to a rougher track. This is the Pennine Bridleway (PBW). Follow the distinct and waymarked PBW for 2.5km until it joins London Road at a T-junction. Turn **R** and follow London Road for nearly 4km until you hit the tarmac road at Mankinholes.

2 Turn **R** and follow the road for 500m. The road turns sharply right, then sharply left: at the sharp left go **SA** down narrow singletrack. Upon joining the road at the bottom go **SA** for approx. 1km. At the end it becomes tarmac double track and descends. When the double track ends, take the rough singletrack on the **LH** side (almost **SA** really) down to a gate and a stream crossing. Ride through shallow stream, climb briefly up the other side and then head **L** down wide track to canal.

3 Turn **R** along canal path for 2.5km until you reach the Stubbing Wharf pub. Turn off the canal, turn **L** and after 25m you'll meet the main road. Turn **L** on road. After approx. 200m (**before** you go under the railway arches) take the road off to your **R**. After climbing this road for 500m turn **R** up a steeper road. Keep climbing up this steep, zigzag farm track. Towards the end you'll pass by a bench and a lovely view on the left. Eventually you reach a flat point at a T-junction with another farm track; turn **L**.

4 After 300m this farm track meets a T-junction with another farm track (the Pennine Bridleway). Turn **R** and climb up the PBW for 750m until you meet the road. Go **L** on the road for approx. 50m, then turn **R** between the houses along the signposted PBW. The PBW climbs briefly before descending steeply to the farmhouse at Shaw Bottom.

5 Turn **L** on farm track for 200m to meet road near New Delight pub. Turn **R** and follow road over Jack Bridge, past Colden School and on for approx. 750m towards Slack. After descending through Popples Common head over to the end of the last terraced house in the row on your **R** and take the narrow, walled-in, signposted bridleway. Keep on obvious singletrack for 400m, keeping wall on your left toward the end. As you meet tarmac keep **SA** and steeply climb for 300m to reach benches and road at top of Lumb Bank.

6 Turn **R** down road into cobbled village of Heptonstall. After 600m turn sharply **L** (after the pub) and head down narrow road for 150m to a bollarded bridleway on **R**. Head down the narrow bridleway. After 150m it widens to double track. Keep going another 200m until you reach the road at the bottom. Turn **R** down the road. After 800m turn **L** steeply down the old, slippy, cobbled path (The Buttress) into Hebden Bridge.

◀◉◯ Making a day of it

This route can be added to the *Whirlaw Common* route (page 5) or the *Todmorden & Walsden* route (page 15). Link to *Whirlaw Common* by the section of canal towpath between the start of the *Whirlaw Common* route at Rodwell End picnic site car park (SD 956247) and where this route joins the canal (SD 965254). To add on the *Todmorden* route simply continue on that route as it diverges after the canal (SD 965254).

DESCENDING FROM SLACK PHOTO: JOHN COEFIELD

Introduction

This physically and technically demanding route showcases the riding to be had at this far flung end of the Calderdale Valley. There's some truly massive ups. And they're all worth it for the downs. It's got the lot really. Slow, slow, quick, quick, slow. The Todmorden Tango.

The Ride

Starting from the famous Grandma Pollards Chippy the ride begins with a much needed warm up along the canal towpath before heading steeply up Birks Lane. The climbing continues in a relatively demanding manner on bridleway, taking in patches of classic Calderdale packhorse, to traverse the shoulder of Rake End. The slabby packhorse descent down to the Shepherds Rest pub always brings grins. There's yet another pub and yet more packhorse shortly after that (uphill unfortunately). After a splash and dash downhill you're at the canal. Then

the climb begins. Getting up Rodwell End and then up Hey Head Lane is a killer combo. Hopefully you'll agree that the descents to Whirlaw Common and Orchan Rocks are worth it. On the map the next section of road up through Todmorden Park woods over to an unclassified track down to Gauxholme doesn't look like it's worth bothering with. But it most definitely is. The track descent down to the canal at Gauxholme is an absolute belter.

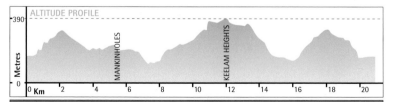

TODMORDEN & WALSDEN   **GRADE: △»▲**

TOTAL DISTANCE: 21KM » **TOTAL ASCENT**: 660M » **TIME**: 3 HOURS » **START/FINISH**: WALSDEN RAILWAY STATION
START GRID REF: SD 932222 » **SATNAV**: WALSDEN » **PARKING**: WALSDEN » **OS MAP**: EXPLORER OL21
PUB: NONE » **CAFÉ**: THE BEAR CAFÉ, TODMORDEN TEL: 07714 333 230

PENNINE BRIDLEWAY ABOVE KNOWL WOOD PHOTO: JOHN COEFIELD

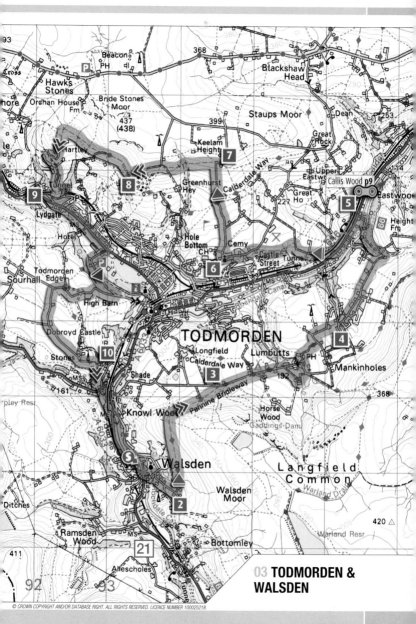

03 **TODMORDEN & WALSDEN**

Directions – Todmorden & Walsden

⊙▸ From Walsden train station cross over the A6033 road and get on the canal towpath behind Grandma Pollards Chippy, turn **R** and follow towpath for approx. 400m to St Peters Gate road bridge over the canal. Turn **L** on road as it passes schoolyard and becomes Birks Lane. Climb up increasingly steep road for nearly 500m to houses.

2 Take walled bridleway (waymarked Pennine Bridleway) on the **L** of final house. Follow obvious bridleway for 2km to join Lumbutts Road near Shepherds Rest pub.

3 Turn **R** along road for 800m then take signposted bridleway off **R** and ride past Lee Farm and Lee Dam to road. Turn **L** briefly along road then turn **R** into Top Brink pub car park. Take walled packhorse bridleway at far end of car park. At end of bridleway turn **L** along road. The road turns sharply right, then sharply left.

4 At the sharp left go **SA** down narrow singletrack. Upon joining road at the bottom go **SA** for approx. 1km. At the end it becomes tarmac double track and descends. When the double track ends, take the rough singletrack on the **LH** side (almost **SA** really) down to a gate and a stream crossing. Ride through shallow stream, climb briefly up the other side and then head **L** down wide track to canal. Pass over canal and follow road around to meet A646 road.

5 Turn **L** along road for 400m then turn **R** under arch (East Lee Lane), then join immediate bridleway and climb up **L**. After challenging 300m climb you reach house at the top, **SA** on to double track farm road. 50m after farm road bends right, turn **L** down bridleway. Follow bridleway for 500m to road.

6 Turn **L** along road for approx 500m then turn **R** up Hey Head Lane (passing golf club entrance after 100m). Climb up Hey Head Lane (steep!) for nearly 1.5km. As road turns sharply right, turn **L** on to waymarked bridleway.

7 Follow bridleway for 700m as it dips down, crosses stream and then rises to join farm road. **SA** on to double track to a gate at edge of a field. **It gets vague briefly here.** From the gate bear **L** off the tractor track and follow **vague** trail (shorter grass). After 50m the trail becomes distinct (sunken singletrack rut). Follow increasingly technical multi-track singletrack downwards to meet bridleway at a gate.

8   Turn **R** through gate and follow obvious bridleway for 1km to reach a gate at the bottom of a dip. Go through gate and climb up **SA** for 200m, as the gradient lessens turn **L** down bridleway alongside wall. After passing Orchan Rocks on your right you'll reach a gate. Go through gate and head down **L** to pass through gate at bottom and on to wider rough lane (Jumps Lane). Follow rough lane downhill as it hairpins a couple of times, enters housing area and eventually meets the main road (A646) at the valley bottom in Lydgate.

9   Turn **L** along A646 for approx 1km towards Todmorden. After passing school turn **R** up road (Ewood Lane) and begin road climb up through Centre Vale Park woods. Upon meeting road at the top of the woods (Doghouse Lane) turn **R** and follow road for approx. 1km, then turn **L** on to minor road (Stones Lane). Follow this road for just over 1km, dipping-then-rising towards an aerial mast.

10   As the road bends right at the mast turn off **L** down un-gated walled packhorse track. Stay on this obvious trail all the way down to join minor road at the bottom. Turn **R** along road for 30m to T-junction with bigger road. Go **SA** across bigger road and pick up canal towpath on other side of the road. Follow towpath for approx. 1km back to Grandma Pollards Chippy and then Walsden train station.

◀ Making a day of it

This route can be extended on to the *Callis Wood & Knott Wood* route (page 9). To add on that route simply continue on that route at it diverges at the canal (SD 965254).

PHOTO: JOHN COEFIELD

Introduction

A popular route but one that is best done during a period of dry weather, ideally with little or no wind. There's a lot of farm track but it's nicely scenic and all quickly dispatched. There's no easy way to get to the top of High Brown Knoll, which ever way you look at it, but when those trails are in good condition, it's a total ripper.

The Ride

The route begins, like a lot of rides do from Hebden, with the climb up Colden Clough to Jack Bridge. It has a horribly steep tarmac start but thankfully calms down after that. It's a great way to head up out of the valley bottom. After passing the New Delight pub you join on to the Pennine Bridleway and follow it on well defined trails and tracks over and down a speedy wide track to Gorple Lower Reservoir. After a period of farm road across New Laithe

Moor you head up over the grassy Shackleton Knoll. The descent down from the summit is steep and rough in places and fast all over. At the bottom is local wild swimming hotspot Lumb Falls. The carry out of the other side and the subsequent ascent up Limers Gates may have you questioning this route's sanity but the return leg back to Hebden Bridge taking in High Brown Knoll's slot-car singletrack and the always-excellent Pecket Well to Midgehole descent will make it all make sense. We promise!

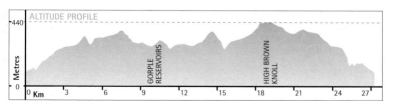

HIGH BROWN KNOLL GRADE: ▲

TOTAL DISTANCE: 27KM » **TOTAL ASCENT**: 700M » **TIME**: 4–5 HOURS » **START/FINISH**: HEBDEN BRIDGE
START GRID REF: SD 992273 » **SATNAV**: HEBDEN BRIDGE » **PARKING**: HEBDEN BRIDGE » **OS MAP**: EXPLORER OL21
PUB: STUBBING WHARF, HEBDEN BRIDGE, TEL: 01422 844 107 » **CAFÉ**: COFFEE CALI, HEBDEN BRIDGE, TEL: 01422 845 629

PHOTO: BENJAMIN HAWORTH

04 HIGH BROWN KNOLL

❺➤ Head out of Hebden Bridge towards Todmorden on the main road. Pass through the traffic lights at the top of a brief rise (Fox & Goose pub on right). **SA** downhill for 200m then turn off **R** and climb up increasingly steep road. As the road turns left after 300m go **SA** on flatter wide track signposted for Jack Bridge. After 800m take the **L** fork uphill and follow track for approx. 1.5km until you meet the road opposite New Delight pub car park.

2 Turn **R** down road for 100m and turn off **L** up farm track (before crossing the bridge). Follow track uphill for just over 1km, passing three farmsteads. Turn **R** after third farm and then after a 50m climb go through gate on **R** into field (Pennine Bridleway). Head down obvious trail, passing through small gate at 250m, to meet tarmac at the bottom. Go **SA** over small hump bridge and climb up steep road for 400m to meet road T-junction.

3 Turn **L** at T-junction and follow farm road (Edge Lane) for 1.2km to gate. Go through gate and climb for 200m to crest of hill, then descend 1km to metal gates at reservoir conduit. Turn **L** after gates and head across Gorple Lower Reservoir dam double track. At end of dam turn **R** down concrete double track for approx. 1km to metal gates. Go through gates and join road.

4 At road turn **L** for 20m then sharply **R** (after the car park) up smooth tarmac narrow road. Go through gate and **SA** for 500m. At track junction turn **R** down slightly loose farm road and descend 500m to a gate on the bridge over the river. Go through gate and follow obvious farm track for approx. 2km. After passing through Walshaw Farmstead fork **L** off obvious farm track and go through gate on to wide track through field. Track becomes more grassy after approx. 300m, just continue uphill alongside wall for another 500m until you reach gate in the wall.

5 Go through gate and head **R** along clear singletrack for approx. 300m to gate. Go **SA** through gate downhill to old farm buildings. At buildings turn **R** down farm track for 125m then turn sharply **L** down rough slightly sunken track. Follow this track down to Lumb Falls. Cross over the falls via the footbridge and follow rooty and rocky singletrack for approx. 50m until the track turns **L** steeply uphill on a sunken walled track. The next 300m uphill is a push/carry up until you reach the road at the top. Turn **R** along road and follow for nearly 1km to meet Keighley Road. Turn **L** and ride road uphill for approx. 1km to a small gate on **R** of the road (it's before bus turning circle layby).

6 Go through small gate and head up increasingly steep singletrack on **R**. The last section on to the top of the hill is a 50m push/carry. Keep following moorland singletrack in the same general bearing for approx. 700m to white trig point. At trig point bear **L** and follow multi-lane singletrack. After 250m the tracks become indistinct to be replaced with wide muddy patch – keep on the same bearing across this patch to meet distinct singletrack on the other side. The singletrack turns **L** and passes alongside catchwater drain. After 50m of riding alongside catchwater drain turn sharply **R** down obvious, rutted singletrack for 800m. After negotiating a rocky stream crossing the track head **L** towards a wall/fence. Keep following tricky, sunken singletrack alongside the fence for approx. 400m.

7 As the fence stops on your left turn sharply **R** (slightly back on yourself) up steep, loose singletrack through heather. Follow the most obvious track for approx. 1.5km as it climbs, then descends, then contours, passing above Allswell Farm. Keep on the obvious track as it bends **R** away from the farm until a gate in drystone wall on your **L**. Go through gate (on to Calderdale Way) and follow waymarked wide tracks down to meet Old Town road.

8 Turn **R** along road for approx. 300m then, shortly before meeting the main road, turn sharply **L** down steep narrow packhorse singletrack for 15m to meet road. **Take care not to exit on to the road before checking it's clear of traffic**. Go **SA** over road and continue down packhorse singletrack. After approx. 200m the sunken walled-in trail opens up; go **SA** and continue down singletrack. After 400m the trail meets a road at the bottom. Turn **L** along road for 1km to meet Keighley Road. Turn **R** down road for 1km back to Hebden Bridge.

STOODLEY PIKE PHOTO: SIM MAINEY

Introduction

This route will not be to everyone's tastes as it's an unusual combination of super steep climbs, green lane cruising and a single bonkers fast 'n' loose descent to finish on. If you want to cover some ground and experience a trio of distinctly different valleys then give it a go. A lot of these trails can be used to access or extend other rides in the area.

The Ride

A gentle station to station warm-up to start. Mytholmroyd to Hebden Bridge station to be exact. Then the pain begins. Wood Top Road and Spencer Lane are infamously steep farm roads. Once past the grumpy Great Jumps Farm the hard work is over and you can enjoy the contouring London Road bridleway. Plain but pleasant sailing for 4km towards Mankinholes. There then follows one the valley's classic climbing challenges. Increasingly steep Permissive

Bridleway packhorse all the way on to the flat top of Stoodley Fell. Ouch. The expansive and starkly bleak descent down to Withens Clough Reservoir on the other side feels like you're dropping into another part of the world completely. From Cragg Vale to Nab End is mostly along green lanes and single track roads with no real significant ups or downs. Your height is maintained all the way until you reach Stake Lane at which point you spend it all in one single glorious kilometre of shattered byway.

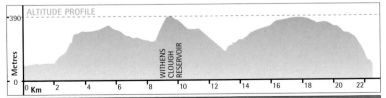

PHOTO: JOHN COEFIELD

05 **MYTHOLMROYD**

Directions – Mytholmroyd

5▸ Exit the train station on to Cragg Road and turn **R**, into Mytholmroyd, passing over canal just before hitting the A646. Turn **L** along A646 for 150m then turn off **L** on to Caldene Avenue. Follow this for approx. 1km then branch off **R** on to Cycle Way.

2 Follow Cycle Way for 800m to meet bollards immediately before Hebden Bridge train station.

3 Turn **L** before the bollards and pass under the railway line. Keep climbing on this bearing, passing to the left of the end house back into tree cover on to cement road (Wood Top Road). After 400m the track turns **R** and exits tree cover. Keep on this farm road as it wiggles through farmsteads as the road turns into very steep cobbles (Spencer Lane).

4 At the T-junction at the top of Spencer Lane have a well deserved rest, then turn **L** to the farmyard. **Don't go into the farmyard!** Push **SA** up the tufty bridleway that's on the **R** of the farmyard to meet a bridleway junction (Jumps Lane).

5 Turn **R** along grassy bridleway for 400m to a ramshackle gate. Go through gate and go **SA** on to farm road for 100m, join Pennine Bridleway, **SA** at crossroads. Keep on PBW (mixed but obvious track **SA**) for 4km to a metal gate.

6 Go through gate and descend 400m towards road at Mankinholes.

7 Before touching the road turn sharply **L** up bridleway (Calderdale Way). After 300m go through gate and head **L** up steep packhorse trail alongside wall. Stay on increasingly steep packhorse trail up to Withens Gate on to the flat top of Stoodley Fell.

8 The track (still Calderdale Way) tilts downwards; stick to the obvious waymarked track down to Withens Clough Reservoir. At reservoir turn **L** and follow minor road for approx 2.5km to meet main road (Blackstone Edge Road, Cragg Road, B6138).

9 Turn **R** along rising road for 2km then turn sharply **L** on to road (Sykes Gate). After 600m turn **R** at farm road with trees at the entrance. After 50m turn **L** down bridleway. After 300m bridleway meets farm track crossroads; go **SA** on to doubletrack farm road. After farmstead at 150m the walled track becomes grassier but still obvious; follow for 400m to gated bridleway on **L** (Water Stalls Road).

10 Go through gate and follow bridleway for 1.5km, keeping on the same bearing as it passes across slightly indistinct fields, passing Pitts Farm just before meeting road (High Stones Road).

11 Turn **R** along road for 500m, then turn **L** down farm road (200m before the pub). Go **SA** for approx. 1km alongside Blackwood Common to meet T-junction bridleway. Turn **L** at junction and pass round Nab End (old quarry full of motocross tracks). Bend **R** and keep on rutted dirt bridleway (Miry Lane).

12 Upon reaching proper tarmac road at the end, turn **R** then immediately **L** and head down Stake Lane byway. Follow this increasingly rough and sketchy track all the way to pop out on to tarmac farm roads. Keep **SA** and follow road back into Mytholmroyd.

◄☜⚙☞ Making a day of it

This route can be added to the *Ripponden* route (page 33). Just after the start of Water Stalls Road (SE 006217) turn **R** down wide bridleway and continue on this bearing for approx. 1km to meet the road (SE 012207). After completing the *Ripponden* route, head back along this same linking section to rejoin the *Mytholmroyd* route.

PHOTO: JOHN COEFIELD

Introduction

A short-ish route and one that is predominantly on rural double tracks and quiet roads. The sections of singletrack encountered on the return leg of the route are really, really good stuff. This route is good for taking a beginner biker out on. Or done as an evening ride if you're an experienced rider.

The Ride

From the dark and claustrophobic main road a quiet track leads you towards Ryburn reservoir and into somewhere much more pleasant. The initial steep dirt climb away from the reservoir isn't exactly pleasant but if you like a climbing challenge it's a good one. Once over the A58 it's a mixture of quiet roads and rural double track that take you past the brooding Great Manshead Hill and over to the hamlet of Lighthazles. The walled-in narrow singletrack comes as something of a pleasant surprise. After a bit more quiet road riding across to Soyland Town the ride finishes with another surprise section of speedy singletrack back down into the dark valley floor.

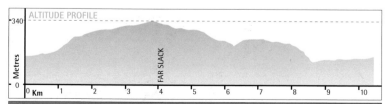

ALTITUDE PROFILE

340

Metres

0

0 Km   1   2   3   4 FAR SLACK   5   6   7   8   9   10

RIPPONDEN **GRADE:** ▲

TOTAL DISTANCE: 10.5KM » **TOTAL ASCENT**: 250M » **TIME**: 1-1.5 HOURS » **START/FINISH**: LAY-BY ON A672
START GRID REF: SE 033188 » **SATNAV**: RIPPONDEN » **PARKING**: LAY-BY ON A672 » **OS MAP**: EXPLORER OL21
PUB: NONE » **CAFÉ**: BRING SARNIES

⊙→ From the main road (A672) head down Bar Lane (near Bridge That Gap sandwich bar).

2 After 1km turn sharply **R** back on yourself (up George Lane). Climb wide, steep, demanding bridleway for 150m to hit tarmac at the end. Turn **R** and head up to A58 road. **SA** across A58 then keep **L/SA** for 150m to Smithy Clough Lane. Bear **L** for 300m then take **R** along double track for 50m, cross over road to farmsteads.

3 After 20m driveway bends left; turn off driveway (i.e. keep **SA**) on to bridleway. Pass by house after 200m, meet road after another 200m (Ripponden Old Road). Turn **L** along road for 200m to T-junction with road (Blue Ball Road). Turn **R** along road for 80m then turn **L** for 500m along wide track (Flight House Road) to join Coal Gate Road.

4 Turn **R** along road as it bends sharply after Greave Head. Approx. 1km after this sharp bend, the road (Ash Hall Lane) bends left, stay on Ash Hall Lane for another 300m after this bend.

5 Turn **R** down walled bridleway immediately before farmstead. At end of bridleway, turn **R** along road for 80m to road junction. Turn **R** along road (Lighthazles Road) for 500m, then turn **L** and follow road for approx. 1km.

6 After Blue Ball Road joins you from the right, take the **L** road (Lane Head Road). After 800m you'll enter Soyland Town; the road bends **R** and becomes Soyland Town Road. Follow road out of Soyland Town.

7 Approx. 100m after the last house (and the village phone box) turn **L** down bridleway. After 250m the bridleway kinks **R** then quickly **L**. 200m after this kink you'll hit houses.

8 Head **R** and down to meet main road (A672). Turn **R** along main road for 2km back to start point.

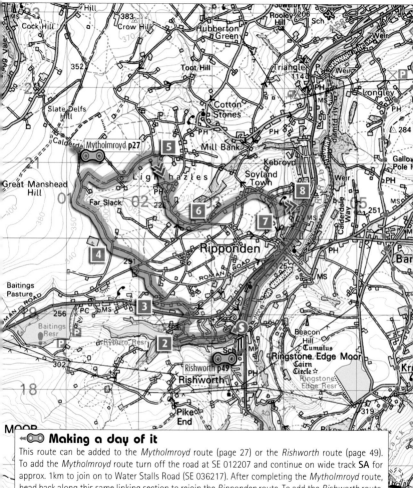

🚲 Making a day of it

This route can be added to the *Mytholmroyd* route (page 27) or the *Rishworth* route (page 49). To add the *Mytholmroyd* route turn off the road at SE 012207 and continue on wide track **SA** for approx. 1km to join on to Water Stalls Road (SE 036217). After completing the *Mytholmroyd* route, head back along this same linking section to rejoin the *Ripponden* route. To add the *Rishworth* route, after completing this *Ripponden* route, simply head up the A672 and turn **L** on to the *Rishworth* route (SE 035179).

06 RIPPONDEN

CLIMBING UP FROM WIDDOP RESERVOIR PHOTO: BENJAMIN HAWORTH

Introduction

A Calderdale classic and must-do route. A truly excellent showcase tour of all that is great about the area. There are some truly epic climbs to conquer but treat the ride like a marathon, not a sprint, and save your best efforts for the technical singletrack highlights as you'll require all your bike handling nouse to get the best out of them.

The Ride

A pleasant spin along the canal towpath acts as a much needed warm-up for the subsequent climb up to Blackshaw Head. The steep and super-fast descent into Colden will test your nerve. The Pennine Bridleway over to Gorple Reservoir sees you covering ground reassuringly swiftly. The climb up from Widdop Reservoir is a classic. It really turns the screw towards the summit. There are two descents you can do from this point: if it's dry the early

singletrack down to Cant Clough Reservoir is a skinny rollercoaster of joy; if it's wet you'll have more fun continuing to blast down the wide and rocky Gorple Road. The climb up to the wind farm and the subsequent road spin along the Long Causeway can test the patience but the generally descending, mostly singletrack, trail network all the way back down to the valley floor is brilliant.

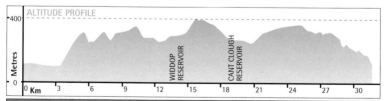

GORPLE ROAD

GRADE: ▲

TOTAL DISTANCE: 32KM » **TOTAL ASCENT**: 710M » **TIME**: 4-5 HOURS » **START/FINISH**: RODWELL END PICNIC SITE
START GRID REF: SD 956247 » **SATNAV**: EASTWOOD » **PARKING**: RODWELL END PICNIC SITE » **OS MAP**: EXPLORER OL21
PUB: NONE » **CAFÉ**: THE BEAR CAFÉ, TODMORDEN TEL: 07714 333 230

Directions – Gorple Road

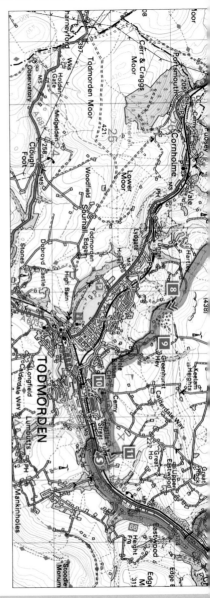

5 Turn **R** out of the picnic site car park and follow road for 200m before turning **L** and meeting canal towpath. Turn **L** along canal towpath for approx. 3km to the barges at Callis Bridge. Turn **L** off the canal towpath after the bridge (but before you get to the barges). Head away from the canal to the road traffic light crossing. Cross over the road and turn **L** along waymarked Pennine Bridleway (PBW). Follow PBW signposts uphill for almost 2km until you meet the Long Causeway road at the top.

2 Go **L** on the road for approx. 50m, then turn **R** between the houses along the signposted PBW. The PBW climbs briefly before descending steeply to the farmhouse at Shaw Bottom. Turn **L** on farm track for 200m to meet road near New Delight pub car park.

3 Turn **R** down road for 100m and turn off **L** up farm track (before crossing the bridge). Follow track uphill for just over 1km, passing three farmsteads. Turn **R** after third farm and then after 50m climb go through gate on **R** into field (Pennine Bridleway). Head down obvious trail, passing through small gate at 250m, to meet tarmac at the bottom. Go **SA** over small hump bridge and climb up steep road for 400m to meet road T-junction.

DIRECTIONS CONTINUE OVERLEAF ▶

07 GORPLE ROAD

4 Turn **L** at T-junction and follow farm road (Edge Lane) for 1.2km to gate. Go through gate and climb for 200m to crest of hill, then descend 1km to metal gates at reservoir conduit. Turn **L** after gates and head across Gorple Lower Reservoir dam double track. At end of dam turn **R** down concrete double track for approx. 1km to metal gates. Go through gates and join road. Turn **L** along road for 1.2km until you reach Widdop Reservoir. Go through the metal gates and ride along the dam head cobbled track. Follow reservoir-side track around and then begin the challenging climb to The Brinks summit (this is all still PBW).

5 At the top of the climb (near some big boulders and a fingerpost) go **SA** along the same obvious track for 1.5km as it rises and falls. After a few 'speed humps' the track bends **L** and after, as the track rises, there are two options, depending on the ground conditions and weather: If it's fairly dry, turn **L** down grassy singletrack (permissive bridleway). **This trail is awful if it's wet**. Follow rutted singletrack rollercoaster for nearly 1.5km until it meets the tip of Cant Clough Reservoir. Follow wide track around right edge of reservoir to the dam head.

> **OR** **Optional Route**
> If the ground conditions are soggy, keep **SA** on the 'speed bumped' wide track (PBW) as it descends for 1.5km, whereupon you turn **L** off and head down the track (still following PBW signposts) to Hurstwood Reservoir. Follow wide track alongside reservoir, bearing away **L** uphill as you reach the dam head. Keep following the obvious track as it climbs up and then descends **R** down to Cant Clough Reservoir dam head.

6 Go through gate and head **L** across dam head double track to gate on other side. Go through gate and follow obvious track (signposted PBW) for a good 2km as it contours, descends, crosses a rocky stream and then climbs amid grassed-over spoil heaps before finally passing over grassy open land and meeting the Long Causeway road.

7 Turn **L** along Long Causeway road for nearly 3km. After road bends around the Stiperden 'horseshoe,' and the road bends left, you turn **R** (almost **SA**) and head down the road towards Shore. After 300m steep road descending turn **L** on to farm road bridleway. After 300m, pass to the **L** of the farmhouse on the narrow singletrack. Follow this bearing, on the most obvious track, for a little more than 2km to a gate at the end of a walled-in section. The track is an entertaining mix of rises, falls, packhorse slabs, rocks, ruts and soggy bits.

8 Go through the gate at the end of a walled-in section and follow stone slab packhorse trail for 200m to a gate. Go through the gate and head downhill passing below Whirlaw Stones on more packhorse trail for 500m.

9 Upon joining a farm road turn **R** and follow double track downhill for 400m. **SA** at track crossroads up a steep, rough, walled climb that levels off after 50m before heading downhill on tight singletrack. After 250m turn sharply **L** up a short awkward walled climb and then descend into golf club car park.

10 **Ride slowly** out of the car park and turn **R** at junction with a road. After 50m turn **L** at the road and follow road for 500m to Bean Hole Head house. Turn **R** after the house down walled bridleway and follow this track for 500m until it ends with a short sharp climb to join a farm track.

11 Turn **R** along farm track, bending **L** after 50m and then after 150m turn **R** and head into farmyard area (watching out for children and animals). Turn **L** in the farmyard and head down walled singletrack that then zigzags you down the hill. Watch out for cars as you enter the picnic site car park at the bottom.

SHIBDEN DALE PHOTO: BENJAMIN HAWORTH

08 **Halifax**

30km

Introduction

Despite being the capital of Calderdale, Halifax never seems to get featured in bike routes. It's not obvious where the good riding spots are, or how to string them together. But it can be done. And it's well worth it. This route is a brilliant example of scratching out some quality mountain biking where you'd least expect it.

The Ride

The immediate comedy cobble climb thankfully gives way to much more tolerable road riding through suburban Halifax and away into the strangely quasi-rural area of Shibden. The rubbly descent down to the Ski Slope (yes, really) is fast and fun. The narrower, swoopier descents that take you down into Shibden Dale are also top fun. Some pleasantly quiet road riding takes you briefly back into the suburbia of Shelf before you pass through the greenery of Royds Hall and a couple of sections of worthwhile off-roading. After passing through Norwood Green and some juicy green lanes and farm trails, being spat out in Hipperholme comes as something of a surprise. Pretty quickly you're whisked away from the traffic and on to the climb up the distinctively ancient Long Lane sunken track. Once at the top of Beacon Hill a great section of technical singletrack links you back on to the comedy cobbles you started on. Riding down the slippy cobbles is no picnic either!

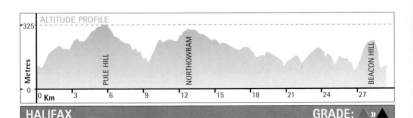

HALIFAX	**GRADE:** △ » ▲

TOTAL DISTANCE: 30KM » **TOTAL ASCENT**: 730M » **TIME**: 4–6 HOURS » **START/FINISH**: HALIFAX RAILWAY STATION
START GRID REF: SE 097249 » **SATNAV**: HALIFAX » **PARKING**: HALIFAX » **OS MAP**: EXPLORER 288
PUB: NONE » **CAFÉ**: BRING SARNIES

Directions – Halifax

⬤➤ Turn **R** out of Halifax train station car park on to the busy road. After 150m turn **R** and descend down Albert Street East road. At mini roundabout turn **L**, and after 50m turn **R** on to Bank Bottom road. After road climbs and bends **L**, go **SA** on to steep closed-off cobbled road. Keep on this cobbled road for approx. 300m until it exits on to tarmac road at top. Turn **R** along road for 50m, then sharp **L** on to Godley Branch Road for 50m, then turn **R** up cobbled road. At top turn **L** and join main road, pass over bridge over the A58, and **SA** over at junction on to Claremount Road ahead.

2 Follow Claremount road for 1.7km to meet A647 road, turn **R** along A647 for 700m, and just before you reach a Bus Stop turn **L** on to Howcans Lane. Follow Howcans Lane byway (tarmac at first then dirt track) for 1.5km to meet cobbles briefly before meeting A647 road. At A647 turn **L** then immediately **R** on to Swales Moor Road.

3 After 200m turn **R** up unmarked path alongside metal railings. After approx. 200m this track ends at a track T-junction. Turn **L** following metal railings. Keep on this obvious track (Ringby Lane) for 1.5km as it descends to meet road opposite Dry Ski Slope. **SA** across road on to cobbled road (Lee Lane), then immediately turn off **R** on to bridleway (Hagg Lane). After approx. 500m at split take the **L** fork.

4 Continue along increasingly wide track for approx. 800m. After passing under pylon lines turn **L** down unclassified road and into housing estate. As road bends **R**, turn **L** on to Calderdale Way Link Path track. Follow this obvious yet varied track for approx. 1.5km until it exits at Shibden Mill Inn pub.

5 Exit pub car park and turn **R** up steep road. **SA** at junction up Howes Lane. The road levels then descends to road junction, turn **L** at junction and follow road for 1km to junction. At junction turn **R** for 50m then **L** on to unmarked track in front of farmhouse. Follow this track. After 300m keep on the wider track as it bends **R**. After another 300m at crossroads with farm road go **SA**. Keep **SA** as track enters a strange truck yard and continue to main road.

DIRECTIONS CONTINUE OVERLEAF ▶

08 HALIFAX

6   At road turn **R** then immediately **L** on to Cross Lane road. At end of Cross Lane turn **L** then immediately **R** on to unclassified dirt road (Bridge Lane). Follow dirt road for 700m until it meets road at its end. Turn **R** along road for 1km into Shelf. At junction with A6036 road turn **L**. After 800m turn **R** into Meadway housing estate (between two yellow brick wall things).

7   Follow curvy road through estate for approx. 700m to a T-junction, turn **R**. After passing Woodside School turn **R** on to Lingdale Road, then immediately turn **R** on to Ancient Highway into Royds Hall. Continue up driveway to meet buildings. At buildings, follow the road **L** passing ivy covered building. Continue **SA** on this road/track for approx. 800m until the now gravel track descends and as it bends **R**, turn **L** off gravel track (over a dipped metal barrier) on to track into Judy Woods. Follow track for 500m to track junction. At junction turn **L** and climb track up out of the woods. **SA** as track becomes tarmac road and continue until you meet A641 road.

8   At A641 turn **R**. After approx. 1km, at pedestrian crossing with a speed camera, turn **R** on to Station Road. Follow Station Road all the way into Norwood Green. Continue right through Norwood Green on this road. The road drops steeply then bends **R** and crosses over Coley beck stream. Continue on this rising road for 400m; as it bends left turn **R** on to unclassified road (Coley Hall Lane).

9   Follow this lane for 1km, passing farmstead at halfway, to meet road at end. Turn **L** along road for 400m to meet A644 road. Turn **R** along A644 for 50m then turn **L** down bridleway. Bridleway narrows, swings **L** and roughens up. Go through metal gate, bend **R** and cross over stream. After stream bend **L** and head up dirt track. Go through metal gate and continue on increasingly more-defined track that descends to farmstead. Bend sharply **L** and descend concrete road. Concrete road rises up and becomes a bit rougher, continue on this road as it joins tarmac, **SA** on towards Hipperholme.

10 As houses stop on your right, turn **R** immediately before a grassy triangle 'land island' and drop down to A58. **SA** across A58 and head steeply down one-way road (Watergate). At bottom of Watergate go **SA** over road on to cobbled road (Station Road). After cobbles change to tarmac and road descends, turn **R** down Badger Lane road. After 400m, mid-hairpin, turn off **R** on to farm road and begin Dark Lane (aka 'Magna Via'). Climb up this ancient sunken track. After approx. 500m narrow track exits on to gravel road. **SA** up gravel road for approx. 750m.

11 As gravel road bends left, with a large drystone wall in front of you, go through the green metal gate on the **R**. Follow obvious track for 500m as it narrows, roughens, bends right, enters trees to finally exit on to road at bottom. At road turn **R** then immediately turn off **L** down unmarked cobbled track (take care if wet!) to meet cobbled road you rode up at the start of the ride. Retrace your steps back to the train station.

PHOTO: BENJAMIN HAWORTH

PHOTO: BENJAMIN HAWORTH

Introduction

Like the Ripponden route in this guide-book, the Rishworth ride isn't a very long route. The Rishworth route contains significantly more exciting trails though, and steeper climbs. The climbs are all about getting to the top in the quickest manner possible (usually road). The descents are all about speed, bike handling and adrenalin. A pocket rocket of a route.

The Ride

A steep and efficient road climb hoists you up past Ringstone Edge reservoir and over towards the M62. After pausing to take in the unusual view of motorway and moorland, it's time to enjoy the excellent singletrack combo of Pike Law and Cock Pit Lane back down the hill. The time difference between how long it takes to get down, compared to how long it took to get up, is amusing. The chunky byway of Heys

Lane gives no warning about the sketchy stone singletrack descent down to the valley floor. Another steep and efficient road climb crawls you up out of the dark valley. Like a remix of the earlier Ringstone Edge up-and-downer, there follows a great singletrack combo. First there's the stoney and splatty track down to Cob Clough and then there's the full-throttle chute past Height Green.

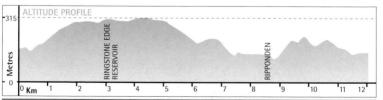

ALTITUDE PROFILE

315 — Metres — 0

RINGSTONE EDGE RESERVOIR

RIPPONDEN

0 Km 1 2 3 4 5 6 7 8 9 10 11 12

RISHWORTH **GRADE:** ▲

TOTAL DISTANCE: 12KM » **TOTAL ASCENT**: 350M » **TIME**: 1–2 HOURS » **START/FINISH**: MALTHOUSE PUB ON A672
START GRID REF: SE 034182 » **SATNAV**: RISHWORTH » **PARKING**: RISHWORTH » **OS MAP**: EXPLORER OL21
PUB: NONE » **CAFÉ**: BRING SARNIES

Directions – Rishworth

➎ From Malthouse head south (away from Ripponden). After 300m turn **L** down Rishworth Mill Lane. Keep on this tarmac road as it wiggles its way steeply uphill, taking the **L** option at any points. After approx. 2.5km you'll reach Ringstone Edge Reservoir.

2 At the reservoir turn sharply **R** along road (B6144). Follow road for 1km then turn **R** on to permissive bridleway. Stay on obvious track for 500m to path junction at Royd Height viewpoint.

3 Go **SA** and follow singletrack around for approx. 500m until it meets road back near Ringstone Edge Reservoir. At road turn **L** for approx. 200m then turn off **R** down Cock Pit Lane byway.

4 At road at end of byway turn **R** down road. After approx. 200m the road bends sharply left; go **SA** at this bend on to Heys Lane byway, splashing through a ford after 80m.

5 900m after ford, turn **L** down walled packhorse bridleway. After bending right the bridleway meets another bridleway side-on (Quakers Lane). Turn **L** down this bridleway for 100m, then turn **R** for 100m passing houses on Holme House Lane to hit the main road (A672). Turn **R** along road for 1.5km into Ripponden.

6 Turn **R** down Elland Road. After 150m pass over the (hidden) river, then take first available **L** on to Old Bank Road/Ripponden Old Bank (also the Calderdale Way). Climb this road for 500m to meet road at the Ripponden Bank Top near pub.

7 Turn **R** along road for 100m then turn **L** on to road (Fiddle Lane). After 250m turn **R** down bridleway. At end of bridleway join road heading **L**, after 500m take farm track bridleway on **R** (Quakers Lane). After approx. 600m this bridleway joins up with where you were earlier. Follow your earlier tyre tracks back to Home House Lane and then the A672. At A672 turn **L** back to the Malthouse.

◀━◯◯ Making a day of it

This route can be added to the *Ripponden* route (page 33): after completing this route, simply head up the A672 and turn **R** on to the *Ripponden* route at the lay-by (SE 033188).

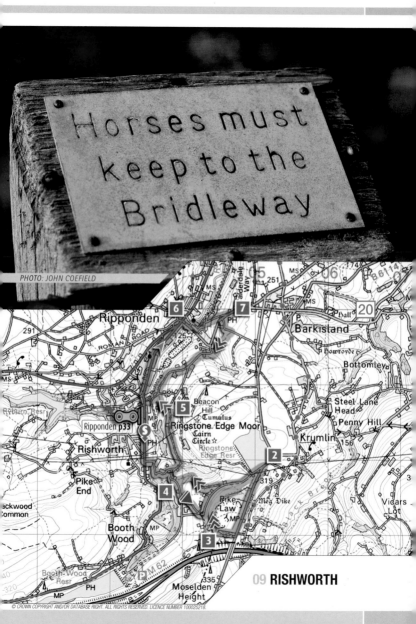

PHOTO: JOHN COEFIELD

09 RISHWORTH

Introduction

The outward leg of this route is a classic example of the local's type of riding. Efficiently uphill on insanely steep roads. Downhill all the way on entertaining speedy singletrack. The return leg isn't quite so extreme. The climb on to the back side of Norland Moor is just-rough-enough. The dinky but tricksy singletrack drop from Longley on to the disused railway line is a nice way to finish this rewarding route.

The Ride

A word of warning: this route starts with arguably the steepest and stupidest climb in the whole book! The road up from Sowerby Bridge to Norland is bonkers. But that type of road is very much a feature of the riding around here. Thankfully the descent down through Pickwood Scar is almost entirely on great singletrack all the way back to the valley floor. Pleasant canal path

cruising takes you past Copley before another challenging climb sends you back up the hill albeit on off-road wide track this time. A usually splatty but entertaining bridleway plops you out above Greetland. Rural double track disappears in vagueness so a bit of compass checking may be required to find your way on to Norland Moor. Some height gain is unfortunately used up on a road descent but the sting-in-the-tail technical singletrack dropping on to the old railway line packs a lot of fun into a short space.

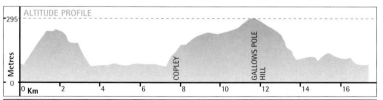

Directions – Norland

➡ From Station Road head up the steep road (Norland Road) with the Police Station at the bottom. After 400m at a T-junction turn sharply **L** up steep road (Sowerby Croft Lane). The road bends right and continues up.

2 At crossroads (with Spark House Lane and Harper Royd Lane) continue **SA** uphill. 800m after crossroads you'll meet road junction at Norland.

3 Go **SA** for 800m and at the second minor road joining from the left, turn sharply **L** down this road then immediately turn off **R** down singletrack (Dye House Lane). After 500m of dirt track descent you'll come out at Pickwood Scar farmsteads.

4 Follow road **L** away from farmsteads. After 150m turn **R** down track (Moor End Lane). After 150m turn **L** down bridleway. Stick to this bridleway for 600m, then pass under railway tracks and bend **L** for almost 1km to meet road.

5 Turn **R** on road, pass over the river, turn **R** and head East on the canal towpath. After approx. 2km of towpath, turn off the towpath (immediately before the Copley bridge) on to road.

6 Turn **R** and follow road away from canal, pass under railway track through tunnel. After the rugby club the road bends right, take the wide track **L/SA** and pass over the river. The wide track bends right and steepens. Climb up this for approx. 500m then turn sharply **L** up wide dirt track for another 500m until it levels off at a track crossroads.

7 Turn **R** at track crossroads and follow wide sandy track for 800m to meet road. At road turn **R** for 100m, then **L** at horsey farmstead (Stockley House) on to bridleway. Follow this straight grassy bridleway for 400m to meet road (Rochdale Road, B6113). At road turn **R** for approx. 1km into Greetland Wall, turning **R** down wide farm road bridleway.

8 Stay on farm road as it bends left (Garden Lane). After 800m the track narrows and grasses over. Go **SA** another 200m and, as wall ends on your left, go **R** through gap in the wall into field. There is no clear track from this point. Head northwest (NW) across field for approx. 200m to fenced standing stone. From fenced stone continue on the same bearing for 80m to wall at field border. **SA** at wall to follow singletrack down to road (Butterworth End Lane). Turn **R** along road.

9 At pub turn **L** down road (New Longley Lane) for 1km to road junction. At junction turn **R**. Follow road (Long Lane) for approx. 300m then turn **L** down stepped permissive bridleway.

10 At bottom of bridleway turn **L** along dismantled railway line for nearly 1km then turn **R** over river to join the main road A58. Turn **R** down A58 for 2km into Sowerby Bridge.

11 Turn **R** before railway arch on to Station Road back to Sowerby Bridge train station.

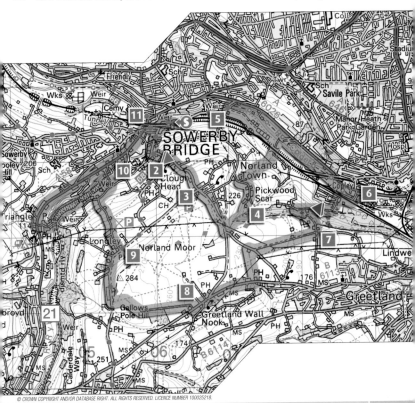

SECTION 2

Bradford Borough

Although it's not the largest in this book, this chapter contains very probably the most consistently great riding of them all. All four of these routes would make it into my Top 10 West Yorkshire routes. Great trails that are always joyous to ride. Surprisingly scenic. Nice vibes.

NEWSHOLME DEAN PHOTO: JOHN COEFIELD

Introduction

This ride takes in some great examples of the gritstone and dirt tracks to be had in this part of West Yorkshire. The two main highlights of the route are Harden Moor and Manywells. Harden Moor is a maze of highly engaging singletrack. Manywells is a superb ribbon of fast dirt with a rocky sting in the tail.

The Ride

The ride begins by heading up Altar Lane, which was an old DH course in the early 90s believe it or not. Once you got the height you encounter Harden Moor, an area stuffed with fun trails criss-crossing across gritstone and dirt. It's well worth an explore in itself. After dropping down towards Haworth you take in the classic Manywells bridleways. One goes up shortly and steeply. One goes down and lasts a lot longer and is a whole heap of skinny fun

with some waterbar leaping action to finish. You continue downwards on wide increasingly shattered road to pass over the river and head into Wilsden. An excellently challenging singletrack climb over bedrock spits you out on to pleasant minor roads to get your breath back. The bridleway descent down to March Cote Farm is a nice mix of the pastoral and speed. The route finishes with some pick-a-ginnel descending through Cottingley before heading along the Millennium Way, via a soggy Beck Foot ford crossing, back to Bingley.

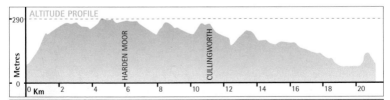

ALTITUDE PROFILE

290 — HARDEN MOOR — CULLINGWORTH

Metres

0 Km 2   4   6   8   10   12   14   16   18   20

BINGLEY & HARDEN MOOR   GRADE: ▲

TOTAL DISTANCE: 21.3KM » **TOTAL ASCENT**: 475M » **TIME**: 3–4 HOURS » **START/FINISH**: BINGLEY
START GRID REF: SE 105394 » **SATNAV**: BINGLEY » **PARKING**: BINGLEY » **OS MAP**: EXPLORER OL21 & EXPLORER 288
PUB: NONE » **CAFÉ**: BRING SARNIES

PHOTO: JOHN COEFIELD

11 BINGLEY & HARDEN MOOR

➎➤ Head away from the bridge on the road for approx. 100m then bear **R** to head up the steep-ish Altar Lane (signposted *Harden Road*). After 1.5km take the **LH** fork and continue with the wall on your left side. After just over 1km you'll join another lane, turn **L** along the lane to meet the road. Turn **L** along road for 500m then turn **R** on to permissive bridleway on to Harden Moor.

2 There are a few ways to cross Harden Moor but the best one is still the most obvious track **SA**. Keep on the obvious track as it passes along the **RH** edge of the moorland. After approx. 2km of this track you'll meet the road. Turn **R** along road then **SA** on to Goff Well Road. Shortly after bear **L** and drop down towards Haworth on road to meet the A629.

3 Turn **R** along A629, then immediately **L** on to unclassified road bridleway (Hardgate Lane). Follow this bridleway (farm road - singletrack - farm road) for 500m to meet B6144. Turn **L** for 1.3km (crossing over A629 at 500m). Turn **R** off B6144 and head up West Manywells bridleway for 800m. As you meet the road at the top, turn **L** for 50m, then cross over the road and take the track on the other side. Follow this obvious track (East Manywells) for 1km, then cross over the road at the bottom and continue down wide broken road (Hallas Lane) as it descends to cross over a river in the valley bottom. Climb away from the river on minor road for 400m (bending through past houses) to meet T-junction with road.

4 Turn **R** along road for 400m then turn sharply **L** (Tan House Lane dirt track) and contour around for just over 1km to enter Wilsden. At the end of Tan House Lane turn **L** along Chapel Row for 200m to meet main road. At the main road turn **L** and then take the second **R** (Smithy Lane) and then join bridleway **R**. After a challenging singletrack climb continue on wide track to a road corner, go **SA** on the road (Cross Lane) and follow it as it bends **R**. 400m after the bend turn **L** off the road down gated bridleway to March Cote Farm. Pass through farmstead and continue on bridleway for 400m to enter housing estate in Cottingley.

5 Find a fun way through the estate and meet the B6266 at the bottom. Turn **L** along B6266 for nearly 1km, then as the road bends right over the river, turn off **L** down the Millenium Way. Follow this obvious track for 1.8km (via the entertaining ford crossing at Beck Foot) to meet the B6429. Turn **R** and follow the B6429 back down into Bingley.

Making a day of it

This route can be added to the *Oxenhope* route (page 67), the *Newsholme Dean* route (page 79) and the *Shipley* route (page 73). To add the *Oxenhope* route, at the top of West Manywells bridleway turn **R** at road, jink over the A629 on to Trough Lane road and join on to the *Oxenhope* route (SE 058352). To add the *Newsholme Dean* route, when you meet the A629 at Barcroft/Cross Roads, turn **R** then **SA** at crossroads on A6033 for 500m to turn **R** on to Vale Hill Lane. Down this steep road, up the steep road on the other side into Oakworth (SE 035388). To add to the *Shipley* route get on to the canal towpath at Bingley (SE 111392) and follow it east for approx. 3.5km into Shipley (SE 139389).

HARDEN MOOR *PHOTO: BENJAMIN HAWORTH*

THORNTON MOOR PHOTO: BENJAMIN HAWORTH

12 Oxenhope

Introduction

This classic route takes in a little bit of almost everything: Stiff road climbs, moorland sheep tracks, ancient multiple-choice byway singletrack, forgotten roads, cruising conduits, mucky fields, scrabbley 4x4 tracks, dipping 'n' ripping walled-in singletrack, heathery play areas and more! It also offers some of the grandest views in the whole of West Yorkshire.

The Ride

The climb away from the A6033 always comes as something of a shock. It doesn't look as demanding as it actually is. Your reward for the grinding up it is the moorland singletrack across Black Moor. The multiple choice lines can lead to some misnavigation but as long as you keep a general bearing you're bound to pop out on the correct road at the end, so don't worry and have fun on there. From Trough Lane and on to Sawood Lane sees some pretty testing tarmac climbing. After a brief super-steep scramble up on to Hambleton Lane it's time to enjoy the multi-lane singletrack fun over to Ogden Reservoir. The lumpy cobbled climb away from the reservoir isn't so fun. A pleasant track alongside Water Board conduit takes you over to the splendid views at Cock Hill. The bridleways of Roms Greave and Stairs Lane offer sporting descents and challenging climbing. The Calder Aire Link singletrack back into Oxenhope is always extremely entertaining.

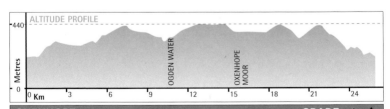

ALTITUDE PROFILE

440 — OGDEN WATER — OXENHOPE MOOR

Metres | 0 Km | 3 | 6 | 9 | 12 | 15 | 18 | 21 | 24

OXENHOPE GRADE: ▲»▲

TOTAL DISTANCE: 26KM » **TOTAL ASCENT**: 525M » **TIME**: 3–4 HOURS » **START/FINISH**: OXENHOPE
START GRID REF: SE 033352 » **SATNAV**: OXENHOPE » **PARKING**: OXENHOPE » **OS MAP**: EXPLORER OL21
PUB: NONE » **CAFÉ**: BRING SARNIES

BLACK MOOR PHOTO: JOHN COEFIELD

12 OXENHOPE

Directions – Oxenhope

➎ From the mini-roundabout head north out of Oxenhope on the A6033 for 1km then after the road bends left take the signposted bridleway off **R** at Royd Wood house. Follow this wide track for 500m as it becomes rougher, then grassy, then double track to the road at the top.

2 At road turn **R** for 500m then turn **L** up bridleway road signposted for *Upwood Park Holiday Homes Tourers and Camping.* **SA** for 500m past Upwood Park to meet metal gate on edge of moor. Go through gate and take the slight **RH** obvious track. After 250m ride over a collapsed drystone wall and the trail splits, take the flatter grassier track **SA** (**not** the singletrack rising off to the right). Follow this increasingly obvious track for approx. 800m to meet gate at road.

3 Turn **R** along road for approx. 1.5km to crossroads with Dog & Gun pub on it. **SA** at crossroads up Sawood Lane. Approx. 200m after passing Coblin Farm you'll come to a gate. Go through gate and **SA** for 200m on tarmac initially followed by gravel fireroad to gate.

4 Go through gate and follow obvious track for 250m to finger posted trail junction. Bend **L** up obvious track to metal gates. **SA** through gates. Keep on this bridleway for approx. 3.5km until you hit road. At road turn **R** and head down to Ogden Reservoir. Ride across the dam head (the *No Vehicles* signs don't apply to bicycles) and climb up cobbled wide track for approx. 2km to gate at The Withens Hotel.

5 Go through gate and meet road, turn **R** and follow road for approx. 3km. After 3km the road bends right; shortly after this bend turn **L** off the road through gate on to permissive bridleway. Follow track alongside conduit for approx. 2km to meet road (A6033).

6 Turn **L** along road for just over 1km then turn off **R** down signposted bridleway (with a bus stop at its start). Follow double track bridleway down for 800m to gate. Go through gate and follow track as it bends left to farmyard gate. Go **SA** across farmyard via a few gates and continue on tarmac double track to meet T-junction with minor road.

7 Turn **R** along road and climb **SA** as the road becomes rough track and goes through a metal gate on to Walshaw & Lancashire Moor. After approx. 800m of climbing you'll reach the Top of Stairs summit and begin descending. **It's easy to descend too far and miss the turn off**: basically after approx. 1km you'll reach a section of recently re-laid cobbled surfacing – as this surfacing ends, haul on your brakes and look for a metal gate through the drystone wall on **R** (signposted *Calder Aire Link*).

8 Go through this gate and follow singletrack alongside wall for 400m, passing through a couple of gates on the way, to exit on to farm road. 50m ahead, at junction with another farm road, turn **R** (following *Calder Aire Link* signs) then at the end of the building on left turn **L** down singletrack. Continue for 1.8km on obvious track as it dips, rises and widens 'til it eventually meets Shaw Lane junction at the bottom. Turn **R** along Shaw Lane and back into Oxenhope.

☞ Making a day of it

This route can be added to both the *Bingley & Harden Moor* route (page 61) and the *Newsholme Dean* route (page 79). To add the *Bingley* route: after crossing Black Moor and meeting Trough Lane road (SE 038352) turn **L**, jink over the A629 and head down the B6429 for 100m to the entrance of Manywells bridleway (SE 064356). After completing the *Bingley* route simply retrace your steps back over the A629 and on to Trough Lane to continue this Oxenhope route. Adding the *Newsholme Dean* route involves a bit of road work: basically stick on the A6033 at the start, pass through Haworth then take Lord Lane (SE 030374) followed by Tim Lane to join the *Newsholme Dean* route at SE 027386.

LOWER FOLD LINK PATH **PHOTO:** *JOHN COEFIELD*

13 Shipley

Introduction

One of the longer routes in this book. This route has ended up being this long because it's impossible to miss any of the best bits out. Great singletrack, fun play areas, scenic green laneing, tough climbs and exciting descents. Shipley Glen itself has enough of a maze of criss-crossing tracks to be worth messing about on all day on its own!

The Ride

A gentle warm up along the canal towpath leads you quickly away from Saltaire and Shipley and up into Thackley Woods. Thackley Woods is a popular play area for local mountain bikers and is well worth stopping by for a muck around on the man-made bits and bobs in there. The natural tracks back down to the canal through Buck Wood are fun too. After passing through the original village where Emmerdale Farm was filmed a lovely track up and through

Spring Wood pops you out near Guiseley. A brilliantly speedy combo of trails shoots you down alongside the golf course and into Baildon. A fair amount of climbing is required to get to the top of Baildon Moor but the views atone for this. The return leg around High Eldwick uses some lovely rural tracks and trails before the final thrilling fling down through Shipley Glen.

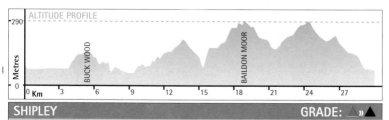

TOTAL DISTANCE: 30KM » **TOTAL ASCENT**: 590M » **TIME**: 3-5 HOURS » **START/FINISH**: SALTAIRE
START GRID REF: SE 139380 » **SATNAV**: SALTAIRE » **PARKING**: SALTAIRE STATION » **OS MAP**: EXPLORER OL21 &
EXPLORER 288 » **PUB**: NONE » **CAFÉ**: BRING SARNIES

Directions – Shipley

6→ From the train station go downhill on the road and get on the canal. Head east along the canal towpath for approx. 3.5km.

2 Turn **R** over canal bridge with white railings and climb up **SA** to a gate with horse-box. **SA** into housing estate. **SA** past houses to main road, turn **L** up main road.

3 As road levels turn **L** up Ainsbury Avenue. After 200m you'll go past a lay-by with Thackley Skills Park, Buck Wood, behind it (feel free to pop in there for a play on the pump track and jumps). Continue along Ainsbury Avenue until it ends at gated Water Authority property.

4 Turn **L** over horse-box and along track for approx. 75m then turn **L** into trees on singletrack. Continue along track for 400m to emerge out of trees on to wider track. Turn **L** along track through Buck Wood for 800m to rejoin earlier track; turn **R** and cross back over canal via bridge with white railings. **SA** on obvious track away from canal which dips then rises to meet A6038 (Otley Road).

DIRECTIONS CONTINUE OVERLEAF ▶

‹⊂⊃ Making a day of it

This route can be added to the *Bingley & Harden Moor* route (page 61) by following the towing path from Shipley (SE 139389) for approx. 3.5km into Bingley and then using brief bits of the B6266 and B6429 to join the *Bingley* route (SE 105394).

13 SHIPLEY

Directions – Shipley continued...

5 Turn **R** along Otley Road for 200m then turn **R** on to Esholt Lane. Follow road for 2km to Esholt village. Follow road as it bends left away from village, after 150m turn **R** along road (signposted *Private Road Public Bridleway*). After approx. 700m bear **L** off tarmac on to wide dirt track. After 300m turn **L** up wide dirt track into Spring Wood.

6 Follow this wide track up right through the woods for approx. 1.5km to pop out at road at housing estate. Turn **L** along road and continue along it for 500m as it degrades to rough road to T-junction with main road. Turn **L** along road for 600m to busy crossroad with A6038.

7 Carefully continue **SA** over A6038 on to rising road ahead (Hawksworth Lane). Climb along Hawksworth Lane for 400m then turn **L** onto narrow signposted bridleway alongside wall. After 100m the trail enters a field, basically continue on the same bearing for 1km until double track meets a surfaced farm road at a junction with a few signposts. Turn **L** along farm road, pass Lunds Farm on your left, continue **SA** descend over golf course path, following the white posts, to footbridge and gate at the bottom.

8 Go through gate and bear **L** alongside lakeside; as main track bends left, take steep vague grassy bridleway climb off **R** for 200m to small metal gate. **SA** through gate up narrow tree lined bridleway. After 250m the bridleway pops out in housing estate; keep on the same path **SA**. After 100m the pathway merges onto driveway road, keep **SA** and join Ladderbanks Lane.

9 **SA** down to a pair of mini roundabouts, jink slightly **R** over them (kinda **SA**) on to Hall Cliffe road. **SA** on road for approx. 300m to proper roundabout in Baildon centre. **SA** over roundabout on to The Grove road. Keep on this road as it bends left and becomes Newton Way. After approx. 600m turn **R** up Hope Lane road.

10 As Hope Lane ends, turn **L** on to signposted bridleway road. Keep on this tarmac for 800m, passing ornate metal gates at a cattle grid and then some houses. At houses the tarmac is replaced by dirt track to a gate junction. Turn **R** through gate and climb narrow bridleway between walls. After 100m follow the bridleway **L** on packhorse trail and follow track alongside the wall. As the gradient levels, and the wall ends on your left, keep **SA** on the track for approx. 400m to meet dirt road near Dobrudden Caravan Park.

11 Turn **R** along dirt road for 1km across open common land to T-junction with Bingley road. Turn **R** along road and descend for 1km (there is an unclassified track on left side of road that's a bit nicer than going down on the road). Turn **L** along Hawksworth Road (with its chevron bend) for approx. 1km, then turn off **L** on to Sconce Lane Public Bridleway.

12 Follow Sconce Lane for approx. 2.4km (bearing **R** at Fairweather Grange Farm at 1.5km) until it meets Otley Road after Weecher Reservoir. Turn **L** along Otley Road.

13 After the road bends right and straightens again turn **L** down tarmac track at the end of the building. After 400m go **SA** through gate on to grassy way. **SA** on grassy way into field, continue ahead on vague track (passing close to telegraph pole) to another gate. Track becomes more defined, follow track to gates at Golcar Farm. Pass by farm buildings and continue out on driveway to T-junction with road (Clovershaw Lane/ Spring Lane).

14 Turn **L** along road for approx. 400m, then turn **R** on to permissive way that runs alongside the road (Glen Road). Then basically follow the paths alongside Glen Road for approx. 2km until you reach houses.

15 Turn **R** down signposted bridleway immediately before The Old Glen House pub and descend for approx. 500m through Trench Wood to pop out on to road at bottom.

16 Turn **L** along road and after it bends right at 800m turn off **R** and head towards the river approx. 150m ahead of you. Push your bike over the footbridge into car park, exit the car park **SA** on to Victoria Road and up the train station.

14 **Newsholme Dean** 11.5km

Introduction

A short but intensely entertaining route. Newsholme Dean is a hidden-away compact micro-valley full of juicy trails and beautiful flora and fauna. As well as Newsholme Dean itself, the skinny trails down into Goose Eye and the stuff back down into Oakworth at the end are excellent little sections too.

The Ride

Slyly avoiding the not-very-busy-anyway roads by slipping along Mill Lane gives an instant idea as to the sort of route this is. It avoids the obvious stuff and takes in little pockets of discreet fun and thrills. The roads, back lanes and green lanes required to get to it involve some unpleasantly steep climbs but they're all firm surfaces so are perfectly manageable. And the scenery and vibe is extremely pleasant. Plotting a route that takes in the best trails of Newsholme Dean involves a bit of criss-crossing over

yourself but it's well worth it. The technical tumbledown trail at the start is a handful. The back way into the Dean off the road on the other side is not so straightforward either. The skinny trail down into Goose Eye is a little slice of mountain bike perfection. The ride finishes with a sneaky little single-track add-on on common land back into Oakworth.

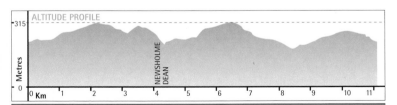

ALTITUDE PROFILE

NEWSHOLME DEAN

Metres — 315 ... 0

0 Km   1   2   3   4   5   6   7   8   9   10   11

NEWSHOLME DEAN GRADE: ◿

TOTAL DISTANCE: 11.5KM » **TOTAL ASCENT**: 320M » **TIME**: 1–2 HOURS » **START/FINISH**: OAKWORTH
START GRID REF: SE 032388 » **SATNAV**: OAKWORTH » **PARKING**: OAKWORTH » **OS MAP**: EXPLORER OL21
PUB: NONE » **CAFÉ**: BRING SARNIES

Directions – Newsholme Dean

⑤ From the crossroads junction of Keighley Road, Colne Road, Providence Lane, Manor Park and Mill Lane, head down Mill Lane (signed *Woodlands 1 to 21 Leading to Mill Lane*). At end of Mill Lane continue **SA** down the bollarded pathway and follow to meet road at end. At road turn **L** and climb for approx. 200m then turn **R** off road on to signposted bridleway double track.

2 Follow bridleway for 400m to T-junction with Turnshaw Road byway, turn **L** along byway for 500m then turn sharply **R** up wide rising bridleway (White Lane). Continue along this for 800m as it turns into tarmac and descends to T-junction with road at bottom. At road turn **L** and descend steeply for 400m, then climb steeply for 400m to signposted bridleway off **R** (opposite Broad Head Lane).

3 Follow tarmac double track bridleway for 300m as it becomes rougher and narrower. As speedy track bends right, haul on your brakes and turn off **L** down clear but unmarked bridleway singletrack between fence and wall. After 100m you reach gate. Go through gate and continue along obvious singletrack, taking care to head down the steep, awkward turn-off **L** after approx. 50m (**Do not** continue along the slightly rising wall-side track). Continue down technical track, over a stream and **SA** down grassy section to gate. Go through gate over to stone humpback bridge over stream. **SA** after bridge for 50m, then bear **R** and go through metal gate on to rising double track.

4 Basically keep on obvious wide track, don't turn off into any farmyards. After approx. 700m the track steepens and bends **L**; continue up this for another 200m to meet road at top. At top turn **L** along road for just over 1km to signposted bridleway on **L**.

5 Head down this bridleway and follow it for approx. 1km until you join on to where you were earlier (point **4** above). **SA** on the same wide track until you reach the spot where the track steepens and bends left, at this point turn off **R** and head down narrow singletrack. Keep going as this singletrack joins a wider track and curls **R** and heads out between houses to meet road at Goose Eye.

6 Turn **R** along road uphill for approx. 1.4km. As you crest over the summit turn **L** on to unclassified dirt road (Race Moor Lane). Dirt track exits into suburbia; continue **SA** on tarmac. At junction with road turn **L** and follow road **SA**, past the end of Dendrum Close on your **R**, and continue **SA** on narrow tarmac.

7 As tarmac surface ends, continue **SA** (ever-so-slightly **L**) on singletrack across grass. Follow singletrack as it descends and then bends **R**, widens and passes a pond. After passing the pond there's a fork in the singletrack; fork **R** down singletrack to join wider bridleway and follow this obvious track as it widens and exits on to road in Oakworth. At road turn **R** and continue **SA** over mini-roundabout and on to crossroads junction where this route started.

◄⊙○ Making a day of it

This route can be added to both the *Oxenhope* route (page 67) and the *Bingley & Harden Moor* route (page 61). Adding the *Oxenhope* route involves a bit of roadwork: head south through Haworth and pick up the A6033 to head up the bridleway at Royd Wood house (SE 039358). To add the *Bingley* route head down Station Road out of Oakworth, turn **L** on the A6033 and descend into Cross Roads. **SA** on the A629 for another 250m to join the *Bingley* route on bridleway (Worth Way) off **R** over to Brow Top Road.

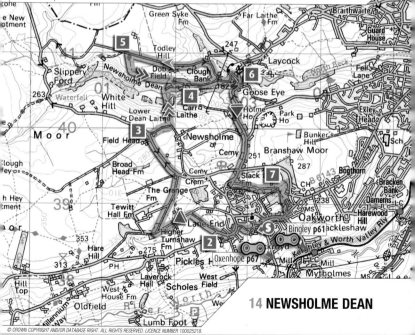

14 NEWSHOLME DEAN

© CROWN COPYRIGHT AND/OR DATABASE RIGHT. ALL RIGHTS RESERVED. LICENCE NUMBER 100025218.

SECTION 3

Kirklees Borough

The terrain, and the riding on offer, on the routes in this chapter is arguably the most varied of all the chapters in this book. There's some beautifully scenic 'Last Of The Summer Wine' rurality and green laneing. There's some singletrack in the leafy suburbs. There's also some ugly-beautiful bleak Pennine moorland.

JOHN HORSCROFT AND HAIGH CLOUGH (ROUTE 18) PHOTO: JOHN COEFIELD

BACK LANE PHOTO: JOHN COEFIELD

15 Mirfield & Dewsbury

Introduction

One of my personal favourite little routes. Partly because it is a revelation to encounter such great little pockets of prettiness amidst an apparently fairly built up part of West Yorkshire, but mainly just because the trails offer such consistently great riding. The latter half of this route has some of the county's best secret singletrack.

The Ride

Starting from Mirfield town centre it doesn't take long to pass the grand old Newhall Mills grounds, and up into some high rural farm lands. Then, just as quickly, you find yourself back in suburbia as you zip through Kirkheaton. Just when things aren't looking too promising you head up the fantastically named Long Tongue Scragg Lane and shoot off along an instantly brilliant piece of singletrack to Houses Hill. After Houses Hill you encounter your first bit of Back Lane. It starts off innocuously enough, but gradually narrows and speeds up to become seriously fun singletrack. The subsequent steep haul up through Whitley Wood is a challenge, but in a good way. After a bit more Back Lane blasting you need to carefully string together three woods (Jordon, Oliver and Hagg) and pass across Dewsbury District Golf Club. There's some excellent twisty stuff to be had in these woods but it's also easy to lose your bearings if you get carried away.

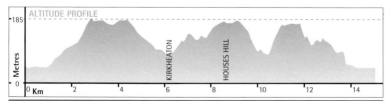

MIRFIELD & DEWSBURY   GRADE: ▲

TOTAL DISTANCE: 15KM » **TOTAL ASCENT**: 375M » **TIME**: 2–3 HOURS » **START/FINISH**: MIRFIELD
START GRID REF: SE 203 195 » **SATNAV**: MIRFIELD » **PARKING**: MIRFIELD » **OS MAP**: EXPLORER 288
PUB: NONE » **CAFÉ**: BRING SARNIES

> Start at Mirfield railway station. Turn **R** out of the station yard, taking Hopton New Road over the river to road T-junction. Turn **L** along road for 400m then turn **R** up Hagg Lane.

2 After 250m at a crossroads turn **R** up iron gated wide tarmac drive. After 200m turn **L** down singletrack. After approx. 200m turn **R** off track through wooden gate. Head **L** up wide gravel track. Gravel stops and track becomes sunken grass track **SA**; continue to pass through metal gate. Bear **L** after gate and head over field for 100m to go through another metal gate. Keep on this bearing for another 50m and a clearer track appears; follow this tufty track uphill, following the fence line for approx. 400m. Join double track at the top and turn **R** to join road.

3 Turn **R** along road for just over 1km then turn **L** down Cockley Hill Lane into Kirkheaton. At crossroads keep **L**, then after 250m turn **L** along main road. After 400m take the **L** fork (Stafford Hill Lane), along another 400m to meet road T-junction, turn **L** for 500m (passing Clay Pit on your left).

4 Take the narrow road up **L** (Long Tongue Scragg Lane) and climb for approx. 400m, then take bridleway singletrack off to the **R**. Follow obvious track for 500m to meet Houses Hill houses. **SA** for 200m to meet road. Turn **L** up road for 800m to meet bigger road T-junction. Turn **R** along road for 500m, passing Hare & Hounds pub, then turn **L** down Back Lane.

5 Pass a red phone box outside a farmhouse, pass through a blue metal gate and **SA** along double track. Double track narrows to singletrack and steepens downhill to meet gates. Turn **R** immediately after gates and dip down over a beck to join tarmac bridleway on other side. **SA** 200m along tarmac then at houses turn **R** and begin climb up Whitley Wood.

6 After a testing climb you'll meet bridleway coming from the left; bear **R** and head down tree-lined 'tunneled' wide track. The track narrows to singletrack and then spits you out on to tarmac. After a brief tarmac section turn off **L** down narrow hedge-lined singletrack. Follow this descending track for approx. 800m.

7 The track levels and passes into a slight clearing with a trail crossroads; turn off **L** into Jordon Wood. Follow rollercoaster tight singletrack on same bearing through woodland for approx. 400m to exit woodland at edge of golf course. Turn **L** briefly then take bridleway track **R** downhill through golf course for approx. 300m, then take **L** track into Hagg Wood. Follow obvious track down through the woods to join tarmac road, go **SA** and rejoin Hagg Lane (near the iron gated wide tarmac drive). Turn **L** and retrace your steps back into Mirfield.

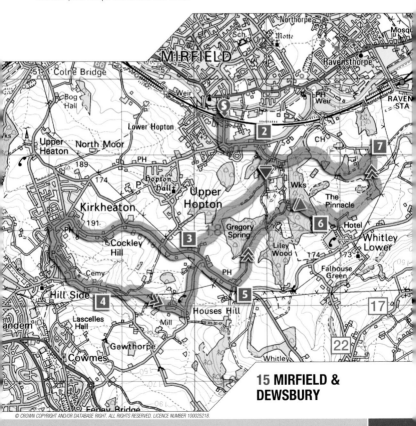

15 MIRFIELD & DEWSBURY

PENNINE BRIDLEWAY ABOVE PIETHORNE RESERVOIR   PHOTO: JOHN COEFIELD

16 Hollingworth Lake

18.8km

Introduction

Technically this route might not actually be in West Yorkshire but it is a great South Pennines classic. Pennine bridleways, reservoirs, the M62, bleak moorland views, broken byways, bypassed hamlets, unexpected singletrack. The West Yorkshire mix is there. Not to mention that distinct sensation of stitching together patches of countryside amidst strips of settlements.

The Ride

Starting from the manmade reservoir of Hollingworth Lake you pass underneath the manmade M62-on-stilts and on to the manmade Pennine Bridleway. As you pass along the easy going and easily navigable tracks, there's a feeling of making your way away from suburbia, civilisation and transport links up away into the countryside. It's a great feeling and one that distills a certain essence of mountain biking into one hour of slow release. After leaving the tarmac at Rakewood, the trails get increasingly interesting and challenging. The outbound leg to Ripponden Road is on swift, wide bridlepaths. A brief but sporting section of singletrack that avoids Denshaw will awaken your bike handling chops nicely. A fast and engaging descent into Higher Ogden will further stir your adrenaline. The broken-up byways from Ogden back to the M62 will give you a full body workout! The last laugh is kept for Deep Lane, an excellent swoopy and nippy track that delivers you back into civilisation with a grin.

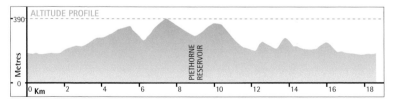

ALTITUDE PROFILE

PIETHORNE RESERVOIR

Metres — 390 / 0

0 Km   2   4   6   8   10   12   14   16   18

HOLLINGWORTH LAKE   **GRADE:** ▲

TOTAL DISTANCE: 18.8KM » **TOTAL ASCENT:** 484M » **TIME:** 2-3 HOURS » **START/FINISH:** HOLLINGWORTH LAKE
START GRID REF: SD 939152 » **SATNAV:** HOLLINGWORTH LAKE » **PARKING:** RAKEWOOD ROAD CAR PARK
OS MAP: EXPLORER OL21 » **PUB:** NONE » **CAFÉ:** BRING SARNIES

Directions – Hollingworth Lake

➤ From Hollingworth head down Rakewood Road on the north east side of the lake for 1.5km. Follow the signpost **SA** on Pennine Bridleway (PBW). Follow PBW under the M62-on-stilts; approx. 1km after the M62 follow the PBW as it turns right and heads uphill on farm track.

2 Go through a gate as the gradient lessens and continue on PBW for 500m to a gated crossroads of wide tracks.

3 Turn **L** and follow wide waymarked track (PBW/Rochdale Way) for nearly 4km, dipping down to Piethorne Reservoir and then rising to meet the A672.

4 Turn **R** down A672 for 1km then turn off **R** down 'gravel mouthed' bridleway. As bridleway joins A640 road at the bottom, turn **R** along rising road for approx. 800m, then turn **R** up byway. After 200m turn **L** at byway junction and follow byway past messy farm with lorries for barns(!) and descend on obvious track to Higher Ogden hamlet.

5 **SA** down road past Bulls Head Pub. Continue along road bearing left, and just before it joins main road (A640) turn **R** down wide road into industrial estate. After road bends right take the cobbled track off up **L** and climb fairly steeply to farmhouses at top of Rough Bank. **SA** through houses for 700m to T-junction with Carr Lane byway.

6 Turn **R** and climb up rough, rocky track (Carr Lane) for approx. 700m to a trail junction. Turn **L** at junction and head down to Tunshill Farm. **SA** through farm and over M62 bridge to Tunshill Golf Club. From golf club car park follow tarmac road **SA**. The road bends sharply right, then curves left.

7 At the farm buildings (approx. 300m after this curve) turn **R** down wide road. Follow road for 300m to a large wide junction of roads and tracks. Take the signposted double track bridleway uphill (fairly **SA**). After 400m go through gates at farmstead and into fields. Keep on the same bearing for 100m or so until a clearer surfaced track appears alongside the wall on your **L**. Get on this track (Deep Lane) and follow it down and around a sharp **R** bend back along to Rakewood Road. Retrace your way along Rakewood Road back into Hollingworth.

16 HOLLINGWORTH LAKE

17 Pennine Bridleway & the M62

17.5km

Introduction

A route of two halves. The outward leg to the M62 can be bleak and baffling. The return leg is weirdly excellent. It's a ride that shouldn't be done in bad weather or during soggy ground conditions. If you find a clear and firm-running day, you'll not regret doing this unique and esoteric route.

The Ride

Heading out of Denshaw on the Huddersfield Road you quickly find yourself entering the bleak Saddleworth moors. If the weather is playing ball, it can be a starkly beautiful, beguiling place. If the weather's grim, it's very grim. This is not a route to do if it's wet. The Pennine Bridleway takes you away from the road and up on to moorland proper. You'll be coming down this same track at the end of the route, undoubtedly in a better mood than when you're heading up it at the start. Heading up the A672 towards the M62 you'd be forgiven for questioning the sanity of this route. This quizzing will continue as you head off the road and on to messy tracks. Then you'll find yourself riding peculiarly alongside the M62 on Windy Hill singletrack and all will become clear. The return leg is along one of the best sections of the Pennine Bridleway with plenty of big ring grinning and multi-track play.

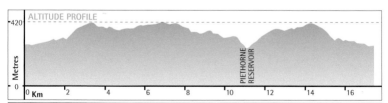

ALTITUDE PROFILE

PIETHORNE RESERVOIR

Metres

420

0

0 Km   2   4   6   8   10   12   14   16

PENNINE BRIDLEWAY & THE M62   **GRADE:** ▲

TOTAL DISTANCE: 17.5KM **» TOTAL ASCENT**: 410M **» TIME**: 2–3 HOURS **» START/FINISH**: DENSHAW
START GRID REF: SD 974105 **» SATNAV**: DENSHAW **» PARKING**: DENSHAW **» OS MAP**: EXPLORER 288
PUB: NONE **» CAFÉ**: OCCASIONAL TEA VAN NEAR POINT 4

Directions – Pennine Bridleway & the M62

➎ From Denshaw take the A640 road east out of the village. After passing between the reservoirs keep on road for another 350m, then turn **L** down gated double track (signposted *Pennine Bridleway*).

2 Follow Pennine Bridleway (PBW) for approx 2.5km, passing Readycon Dean Reservoir, to meet A672 Ripponden Road.

3 Turn **R** along road for 2.5km (watch out for fast cars and ride on the sidepath where you can if you prefer). Go past the Pennine Way and car park lay-by, and after 150m turn **L** up signposted tarmac bridleway towards aerial mast.

4 As track bends right towards smaller mast, turn off **L/SA** on mucky messed-up multi-track past large mast on your left. (Don't worry, there's good stuff ahead!) After approx 250m the mess stops and you pass through a drystone wall on to a better trail. **SA** and after a rise the trail becomes walled-in.

5 **SA** for almost 2km down walled-in track (try and get on the higher-up singletrack option on the right as soon as you can). After the singletrack drops and joins the lower wide track, the track bends **L** to a trail junction.

6 Turn **L** at junction and follow waymarked PBW for approx 2km, passing Piethorne reservoir, to meet A672.

7 From the A672 there are two options: Either cross over the A672 and turn **L** to retrace your steps back to Denshaw via Readycon Dean Reservoir on the PBW.

OR Or turn **R** down the road back in to Denshaw.

⟨⟩◯ Making a day of it
This route can be combined with the *Marsden* route (page 99) with a bit of jiggery-pokery. From Denshaw go past the turn-off to Readycon Dean Reservoir and continue on the A640 to GR SE 003123 and join on to the Western tip of the *Marsden* route. After following the *Marsden* route take the track at SD 998122 up to Readycon Dean Reservoir and continue on this route.

MOSS MOOR

Linsgreave

Way Stone Edge

Way Stone

Buckstones Mo

Buckstones Ho

Windy Hill

M 62

Longden End Brook

Nicholas Pike

Bleakedgate Moor

405

466

White Hill

March Hill

MP

Norman Hill Resr

Piethorne Resr

Great Hill

Readycon Dean Resr

Denshaw Moor

MP

Ogden Resr

PC

Ogden

PH

Cemy

Rooden Resr

367

Pennine Bridleway

Marsden p99

Hotel

338

Crook Gate Resr

Dowry Resr

MP

Castleshaw Moor

Slences

391

Crompton Moor

272

Denshaw

New Years Bridge Resr

Broadhead

95

97

99

01

Crompton Fold

Broshes

17 PENNINE BRIDLEWAY & THE M62

WILLYKAY CLOUGH & MARSDEN PHOTO: JOHN COEFIELD

18 Marsden & Willykay Clough

18km

Introduction

A challenging climb out of Marsden on steep roads and broken byway leads to a fast and loose descent into Merry Dale. The cobbled climb that follows is a challenge for the legs. The road bash along the A640 is a challenge of patience, but the fabulous mixed-up singletrack of Willykay Clough is the pay-off.

The Ride

A pleasant warm up on minor road and canal towpath is much needed to get your body prepared for the stiff climb up on to Booth Bank. The byways of Green Lane and Scout Lane appear innocent on the map but on the ground are actually rather testing sections of real off-road riding. Green Lane is a scrambley climb. Scout Lane is a loose and speedy descent followed by a gut busting cobble climb out of the other side. The section along the A640 is a necessary evil, although passing across Blacker Edge above March Haigh has a certain broody appeal. Buckstones car park is an alternative start point if you want to break up the tarmac. The main reason for riding this route is the highly entertaining singletrack of Willykay Clough. A lengthy and uninterrupted moorland singletrack path of dips, ruts, humps and jumps. It is surprisingly worthwhile even in wet weather too.

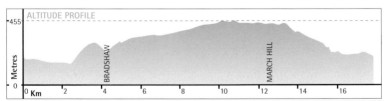

MARSDEN & WILLYKAY CLOUGH **GRADE:** ▲

TOTAL DISTANCE: 18KM » **TOTAL ASCENT**: 370M » **TIME**: 2–3 HOURS » **START/FINISH**: MARSDEN (OR BUCKSTONES CAR PARK SE 017136) » **START GRID REF**: SE 047118 » **SATNAV**: MARSDEN » **PARKING**: MARSDEN RAILWAY STATION **OS MAP**: EXPLORER 288 » **PUB**: NONE » **CAFÉ**: BRING SARNIES

Directions – Marsden & Willykay Clough

🡆 From Marsden Railway Station follow Station Road around and then **SA** on Warehouse Hill Road; after 300m get on to the canal towpath. Follow towpath east to bridge 51.

2 At bridge 51 go on to the road, pass over the canal and turn **R**, under railway bridge and head up Booth Bank. After a steep 200m climb turn **L**, up more steep stuff for approx. 200m to meet Green Lane junction. Turn **R** up Green Lane for 400m to meet road.

3 Turn **R** along road for 500m to crossroads near Rose & Crown pub. **SA** down Scout Lane – as the road bends right, go **SA** and descend down increasingly steep, loose track to a bridge at the bottom (Merry Dale). Continue up steep cobbled climb ahead to join road (Bradshaw Lane).

4 Turn **R** along road for 500m then turn off **L** at a small 'triangle island' junction. Follow minor road (Burnt Plats Lane) for approx. 2km to meet A640.

5 Turn **L** along A640 for 5.5km (passing Buckstones car park at 3km – possible Alternative Start), then turn **L** at Pennine Way.

6 Almost immediately fork off **L** on less distinct track (the footpath sign is incorrect, it's a bridleway). Keep on this entertaining track, through a stream crossing at 2.5km, down a rocky section to a bridge at the bottom. **SA** over bridge and climb shallow steps to road.

7 Follow road (Waters Road) for 2km to Marsden and take the road over railway tracks just before Marsden Railway Station.

🔗 **Making a day of it**

This route can be combined with the *Pennine Bridleway & the M62* route (page 95) with a bit of jiggery-pokery. At SE 003123 stay on the A640 for another 400m and then turn **R** up track at SD 998122 up Readycon Dean Reservoir and on to the the *M62* route. On the return leg, after Readycon Dean Reservoir retrace your tracks back on to this Marsden route at SE 003123.

This route can also be combined with the *Meltham* route (page 103) near the middle of Marsden on the Station Road/Warehouse Hill Road junction at SE 049117.

18 MARSDEN & WILLYKAY CLOUGH

LANE CRUISING ABOVE DIGLEY RESERVOIR PHOTO: JOHN COEFIELD

19 Meltham

Introduction

This is a really pretty ride. It takes in plenty of 'Last Of The Summer Wine' style scenery. It's one of the more rolling green and consistently rural feeling routes in this guidebook. But it's not just a scenic ride for glorified touring bikes. It also offers a decent share of challenging bits where a decent mountain bike is a must-have.

The Ride

The road out of Marsden starts out impressively straight and suitably steep; it's a pleasingly efficient way of gaining height and getting out amidst increasing rurality. An amusingly short and sweet rocky drop past the Whitehouse Pub breaks up the tarmac bashing. The off-road detour around Meltham Grange minimises the tarmac and maximises freewheel zipping down speedy field tracks. After passing through Meltham on scary-fast roads it's time to haul on the brakes and begin the haul up on to pretty Meltham Moor. A real climbers challenge. A modest 'green lane' loop down to Digley Reservoir is well worthwhile. The final flourish of this route is the big ring grins to be had down Wessenden reservoirs valley. The first half is a lovely stretch of curves and swoopy bits. The latter half is wider and can either be cruised or attacked, depending on your mood.

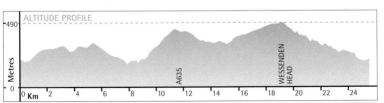

MELTHAM **GRADE:** ▲»⁄

TOTAL DISTANCE: 25KM » **TOTAL ASCENT**: 600M » **TIME**: 3-4 HOURS » **START/FINISH**: MARSDEN
START GRID REF: SE 047118 » **SATNAV**: MARSDEN » **PARKING**: MARSDEN RAILWAY STATION » **OS MAP**: EXPLORER 288, EXPLORER OL21, EXPLORER 277 » **PUB**: NONE » **CAFÉ**: BRING SARNIES

Directions – Meltham

➊ From Marsden Railway Station follow Station Road around and as it bends right to Peel Street, take the **L** along Brougham Road. At end of Brougham Road go **SA**, across A62 (Manchester Road), and start Meltham Road climb. Follow road for approx. 2.5km to reach The Whitehouse pub.

2 At pub, bear **L** off the road down increasingly rough double track. As you join road at the bottom, turn **R** along road to rejoin main road (Slaithwaite Road). Turn **L** along road for 1km then turn **R** down wide bridleway farm road (Deer Hill End Road). After nearly 1km turn **L** through double metal gates.

3 Follow wide track down edge of field until you meet a gated T-junction after 800m. Turn **L** down track and keep **SA** as it becomes a road. Keep **SA** and meet main road, turn **R** and follow road down through Meltham.

4 Immediately after passing over the river, as the road begins to rise, turn **R** in to Royd Road. Follow this minor road. At 1.2km bend **R** and follow road past Royd Farm. This road bends **L** to Ash Royd Farm.

5 At farm the road stops, **SA** up grassy field track (Magdalene Road). Continue up challenging moorland to meet A635.

6 Turn **R** then immediately **L** down double track (with a wide wooden gate near its start). After 800m turn sharply **L** and continue along obvious track (Nether Lane). Follow this 'green lane' **SA** for almost 3km until it meets tarmac road (Acres Lane).

7 Turn **L** up the road for just over 1km to meet the A635 again. Turn **L** and follow A635 for approx. 2.75km to a junction.

8 Turn sharply **R** down road (Wessenden Head Road). Follow road for 300m then turn **L** down double gated double track (Pennine Way). Follow obvious track down alongside reservoirs. After the fourth reservoir the track meets a road; make your way on roads, generally **SA**, back into Marsden.

⚙️➤◯ᗞ Making a day of it

This route can also be combined with the *Marsden & Willykay Clough* route (page 99) near the middle of Marsden on the Station Road/Warehouse Hill Road junction at SE 049117.

19 MELTHAM

SECTION 4

City of Leeds Borough

There's nothing better than finding great mountain biking within a stone's throw of a major city. There's not a lot of obvious hills around Leeds but there's still some excellent riding to be had. The industrial-remote confined-open juxtaposition of the other boroughs is replaced with a milder mix of low-lying suburbia and rurality. There are plenty of singletrack gems to be unearthed between the housing estates and the stately homes.

BLACK CARR WOODS (ROUTE 20) **PHOTO**: JOHN COEFIELD

20 Pudsey

10.8km

Introduction

This modest looking route is an absolute belter. It's not an all day affair by any means but as a half-day or evening blast it's er... a blast. Starting from the unlikely confines of Pudsey surburbia you're quickly hurtling off down some genuinely excellent off-road riding amidst a pretty rural feeling landscape.

The Ride

Starting from the gates of the impressive Fulneck Moravian Settlement, a village founded in 1744 by members of the Moravian Church, head along the road through suburbia towards Pudsey. A speedy and swoopy descent takes you away from the suburbs and down into the juicy confines of Black Carr woods and The Bank. A fairly stiff climb takes you almost all the way back to where you started but then you shoot off down a great little up 'n' downer track called Keeper Lane. After a brief jink

through Tong village you encounter the excellent cresta run trail called Springfield Lane. Following a thankfully brief blast on the A58 you turn off into Upper Moor Side. Keep a beady eye out for the easily missed trail down into Cockers Dale and Tong Beck. You don't want to miss it because it's a fabulous and unexpected tree-lined single-track delight.

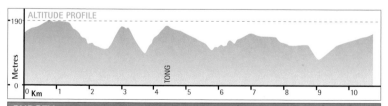

ALTITUDE PROFILE

190

Metres

0

0 Km   1   2   3   4   TONG   5   6   7   8   9   10

PUDSEY   **GRADE:** ▲ » ▲

TOTAL DISTANCE: 10.8KM » **TOTAL ASCENT:** 260M » **TIME:** 1.5–2 HOURS » **START/FINISH:** FULNECK
START GRID REF: SE 224323 » **SATNAV:** FULNECK » **PARKING:** FULNECK MORAVIAN SETTLEMENT » **OS MAP:** EXPLORER 288
PUB: NONE » **CAFÉ:** BRING SARNIES

Directions — Pudsey

➎ Head out of Fulneck on to Fartown road; turn **L** up Fartown road for approx. 1km, and after the road bends right (and becomes Greenside road) take the next road **L** (Smalewell Road). After approx. 400m turn **L** immediately before Fox & Grapes pub down bollarded bridleway.

2 Keep on the wider obvious track for 700m to junction of streams at the bottom. Take permissive bridleway alongside stream out of the woods on increasingly wide track for 400m. As the track bends right, turn **L** on to bridleway beginning with small metal footbridge.

3 Climb up this bridleway for 400m to road at top with The Bankhouse pub up on the left. Go **R** along road for 200m then turn **R** immediately before blue sign (*Moravian Settlement Private Road*) down paved track at end of houses. At end of short paved track go **SA** and continue down narrowing bridleway for 400m to bottom. Track widens and bends **R** to stream. Cross stream and head **R** up wide bridleway (Keeper Lane) for 700m to enter housing area. **SA** for 250m to meet road.

4 Turn **L** along road for 250m then turn **R** down Springfield Public Bridleway. After 250m go **SA** down narrow track. After 600m join wider track at the bottom bending **R** and follow to farmstead. Pass farmstead and bear **L**, follow road 300m to meet A58.

5 Turn **L** along A58 for 1km, then turn **L** at traffic lights heading for Farnley (on Back Lane). Follow road for 200m then turn sharply **L** down wide bridleway. After 250m take bridleway on **R** with metal motorbike-stopper at entrance. Stay on the clear bridleway for 1km to meet road.

6 Cross over road and on to Roker Lane road. Follow this road for almost 2km back to Fulneck.

◀◉◉ Making a day of it

At the north-west corner of this route (SE 213327) you're only about a mile away from the southern end of the *Airedale* route at SE 203343 (page 115). Combining the two routes makes for a decent day ride.

PHOTO: JOHN COEFIELD

20 PUDSEY

© CROWN COPYRIGHT AND/OR DATABASE RIGHT. ALL RIGHTS RESERVED. LICENCE NUMBER 100025218.

21 Airedale

10.8km

Introduction

Like the terrier of the same name, Airedale is a small but frisky place to mountain bike. What it lacks in all out mileage it more than makes up for in play areas. Calverley Woods and Ravenscliffe Woods are criss-crossed with fun little micro-trails and just-because mini-detours. It's well worth heading out a bit further and including the super singletrack of Shell Lane too.

The Ride

From Apperley Bridge it doesn't take long to get on to dirt. Calverley Wood is a well known bikey play area for Airedale locals. There are a lot of spots to mess about on, but that sort of riding is best saved until the return leg of this route. As you head south along the Leeds Country Way dirt track you'll continue to notice fun little bits off to the side of the main trail; these are well worth a play if you fancy the look of any of them. A hectic kilometre along the A647 reminds you that you really aren't far from Leeds city. Thankfully you leave that behind and chug along Priesthorpe Lane green lane, before suddenly splintering off on to the excellently engaging singletrack of Shell Lane. If you still have the time and inclination, which you will, take some time to explore Calverley Wood before heading back to Apperley Bridge with a big grin on your dirty face.

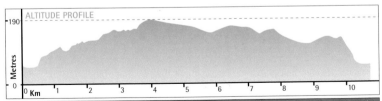

ALTITUDE PROFILE

Metres — 190 / 0

0 Km 1 2 3 4 5 6 7 8 9 10

AIREDALE

GRADE: ▲ » ▲

TOTAL DISTANCE: 10.8KM » TOTAL ASCENT: 195M » TIME: 1.5-2 HOURS » START/FINISH: APPERLEY BRIDGE
START GRID REF: SE 196383 » SATNAV: APPERLEY BRIDGE » PARKING: STANSFIELD ARMS PUB » OS MAP: EXPLORER 288 » PUB: STANSFIELD ARMS, APPERLEY BRIDGE, TEL: 0113 250 2659 » CAFÉ: BRING SARNIES

Directions — Airedale

↪ From Stansfield Arms pub car park (please don't park here without giving the pub some patronage) turn **R** down the A658 for approx. 200m, then turn **L** on to road (Calverly Cutting) and head into woodland.

2 Upon reaching trail crossroads turn **R** along permissive bridleway for 800m to meet A657 road side-on.

3 **SA** across A657 on to Ravenscliffe Road for 200m, then **SA** down Leeds Country Way track. Follow obvious waymarked dirt track for 2km to join tarmac road with industrial site on your left. **SA** along road for 1km to T-junction with road.

4 Turn **L** along road for 300m to meet busy A647. Turn **L** along A647 for approx. 1km, turn **L** (first exit) on the roundabout (signposted *A6120*).

5 After passing under white footbridge take road on **L**. As road turns left into school, go **SA** on Priesthorpe Lane bridleway. After 1.2km (just as the track becomes double track) turn **L** down easy-to-miss signposted bridleway (opposite vegetable field). After 150m go **SA** across wide track (Priesthorpe Road) on to narrower bridleway (Shell Lane). After 800m exit bridleway into housing estate. Turn **R** and follow road for 250m to bollards at end.

6 Go through bollards on to road, turn **L** along road for 1.5km as it bends through Calverley. Pass the New Inn pub on your right. After approx. 150m turn **R** on to forest road byway (not-quite-opposite Clover Crescent).

7 Follow byway into woodland, going through arch at 300m and descend down to where you were earlier (at point **2** above). Retrace your steps back to Stansfield Arms pub.

◄⊙◯◯ **Making a day of it**

At the southern end of this route (SE 203343) you're only about a mile away from the north-west corner of the *Pudsey* route (SE 213327) – page 111. Combining the two routes makes for a decent day ride.

21 AIREDALE

LEEDS COUNTRY WAY AND BARNBOW WOODS PHOTO: JOHN COEFIELD

22 Elmet Cruising

18km

Introduction

A gentle but extremely pleasant ride that can act as a great introduction to mountain biking for some, or it could even be knocked out on a cyclocross bike. Minimal climbing. Mostly green lanes, but with a bit of skinny stuff to spice it up now and again.

The Ride

Starting from Aberford you'd never guess you were only a few hundred metres from the A1(M). From Aberford it's plain sailing, or rather green lane cruising, all the way to Garforth Golf Club along the undemanding but pretty Parlington Lane track. Carefully crossing over the golf course along a suitably short-grassed track takes you to a fun section of smooth but swoopy singletrack. From there you get on to the Leeds Country Way dirt track and follow it as it alternates between hedge lined narrow path and wider farm track to pop out at Scholes village.

The section along the A64 is usually not too busy unless you encounter it at commuting hour. The bridleway down through Becca Home Farm into Aberford is another mix of wide farm road and narrower dirt track with only one real navigational pause to interrupt your cruising.

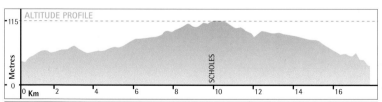

ALTITUDE PROFILE

Metres — 115 — 0

Km 2 4 6 8 10 12 14 16

SCHOLES

ELMET CRUISING GRADE: ▲

TOTAL DISTANCE: 18KM » **TOTAL ASCENT**: 100M » **TIME**: 1.5–2 HOURS » **START/FINISH**: ABERFORD
START GRID REF: SE 434375 » **SATNAV**: ABERFORD » **PARKING**: PLENTY OF SPOTS IN ABERFORD » **OS MAP**: EXPLORER 289
PUB: NONE » **CAFÉ**: BRING SARNIES

Directions – Elmet Cruising

1▸ Head south along main road out of Aberford. Turn **R** up bridleway with phone box at its start (opposite Lotherton Lane). Follow this track to a tunnel at 1.5km. Either ride through the tunnel for 75m or take the 'chicken run' path along the **L** of the tunnel. Continue along track (Parlington Lane).

2 Go **SA** over road at 2.5km and continue along Ellis Lane past Willow Park Farm into golf course grounds. Continue along grassed over track, across golf course, and **SA** along narrow singletrack to meet T-junction with Leeds Country Way (LCW).

3 Turn **R** and follow LCW for 2km until you meet the road at Scholes.

4 Go **SA** and bear **L** into Scholes village centre. Keep on this road to meet the A64 approx. 500m after exiting Scholes.

5 Turn **R** along A64 for 5km. After passing Woodlands Farm take the bridleway off **R**.

6 Follow bridleway down, through Becca Home Farm, to meet a gate at a wood. Go through gate and **SA**, following the arrows to a trail junction.

7 Turn **R** along waymarked bridleway and stick to this track until you pop out in Aberford.

◄○○ Making a day of it
Halfway along the section of the A64 at Saw Wood (SE 391392) you can join on to the southern end of the *Bardsey* route (page 123) and head off into a much more challenging ride.

22 ELMET CRUISING

BRANDON LANE PHOTO: JOHN COEFIELD

23 Bardsey

Introduction

Just a little further north above Elmet (page 119) lies Bardsley-cum-Rigton. It doesn't have much more elevation than Elmet but it has signifcantly more proper mountain biking on offer. The singletrack is generally quite brief but it's of a very high standard. There's sneaky spits and spats of it all over this entertaining route.

The Ride

Warm up along the pleasant minor roads through Scarcroft and the wide dirt track of Kennels Lane before hustling your way along the root and swoopy woodland singletrack alongside Milner Beck. After a nippy section of double track, bookended by bits of tarmac bashing, you head off into Saw Wood on an entertainingly hemmed in narrow track. The route then takes you on a patchwork of estate ginnels, sneaky singletrack and obscure back roads to present to you a real gift of a trail – Brandon Lane. Brandon Lane looks like a dull straight track on the map. On the ground it's a tight and curvy piece of engulfed singletrack threading its way at speed between hedgerows. Great stuff. The return leg back to Bardsley can be done entirely via the Leeds Country Way with its mix of farm road and field. But it's much more fun to nick off down the pocket rocket singletrack to Rigton Moor Farm.

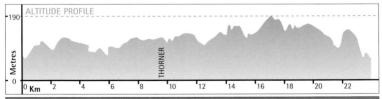

ALTITUDE PROFILE

Metres — 190 — 0

THORNER

0 Km 2 4 6 8 10 12 14 16 18 20 22

BARDSEY **GRADE:** ▲»▲

TOTAL DISTANCE: 24KM » **TOTAL ASCENT**: 120M » **TIME**: 2–3 HOURS » **START/FINISH**: BARDSEY
START GRID REF: SE 369434 » **SATNAV**: BARDSEY » **PARKING**: PLENTY OF PLACES IN BARDSEY » **OS MAP**: EXPLORER 289
PUB: NONE » **CAFÉ**: BRING SARNIES

PHOTO: JOHN COEFIELD

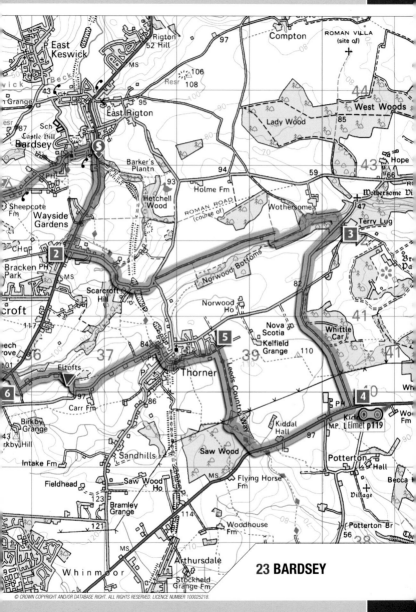

23 BARDSEY

Directions – Bardsey

1 From Bardsey head south along A58 into Scarcroft. At crossroads turn **L** down Thorner Lane.

2 Follow Thorner Lane for 1.5km. At 'triangle island' junction (after passing Scarforth Liveries) take **L** option for 50m to meet start of Kennels Lane bridleway. Follow obvious track for 2km whereupon it turns **R** down edge of field and into the trees. Follow singletrack **L** for 500m to meet bridleway junction; turn **R** up bridleway climb. After 350m turn **R** down wide track before steep scrabbly climb to the road.

3 Turn **R** along road for 1km and, as the road bends right, turn off **L** on double track bridleway (Mangrill Lane). Follow double track for 1.8km to meet A64.

4 Turn **R** along A64 for 1.3km then at a lay-by turn **R** down singletrack bridleway into Saw Woods (Leeds Country Way). Follow this track for 1.5km to meet houses at Thorner.

5 Turn **L** along road for 200m then take singletrack **SA** as the road bends right. Singletrack hits tarmac; continue ahead to meet main road. Go **SA** across main road and follow road (Carr Lane) for 1.7km. As road bends left, take narrow track off **R** with green metal post at the start. After 300m singletrack hits wide track at Eltofts House. **SA** on to Eltofts Farm (after 400m) then at track T-junction turn **R** for 250m to meet A58.

6 Turn **L** along A58 for 70m then turn **R** on road (Stony Lane) for 300m to T-junction with road. Turn **R** along road for approx. 300m; as road bends right, turn off **L** on road (Brandon Crescent). Follow road for 1.2km to T-junction, turn **L** at junction and follow road for approx. 400m as it bends right at houses and then meets road T-junction. Go almost **SA** (slightly to your **L**) on to bridleway (Brandon Lane); follow track for almost 1km to road at bottom.

7 At road go almost **SA** (slightly to your **R**) down Forge Lane road. Keep on this road for just over 1km then turn **R** on to gated bridleway (signposted *Leeds Country Way*). After 2km go through gate at end of track over field and turn **R** down narrow bridleway. After 300m meet road. Turn **L** along road for 200m then turn sharp **R** on to road (Spear Fir). Follow road for 700m to T-junction with road. Turn **L** along road for 2km back into Bardsey.

◀ ⊙⊙ Making a day of it

This route can easily be bolted on to the *Elmet Cruising* route at SE 404397 (page 119) to make a longer day ride. Or if you want to soak up some lovely Stately Home scenery, head west along the Leeds Country Way after Wike (SE 331428) into Harewood House grounds for an out-and-back addition on easy going tracks.

top tens

Here's my pick of the best ups and downs in West Yorkshire

Top Ten Climbs

1. Orchan Rocks *(Route 1)*
2. Horsehold *(Route 2)*
3. Rake End *(Route 3)*
4. Colden Clough *(Route 4)*
5. Old Chamber *(Route 5)*
6. Stoodley Fell Permissive Bridleway aka The Penny Steps *(Route 5)*
7. Gorple Road *(Route 7)*
8. Dark Lane *(Route 8)*
9. Boggart Lane *(Route 10)*
10. Thornton Moor *(Route 12)*

Top Ten Descents

1. Whirlaw Common & Rodwell End *(Route 1 & 7)*
2. Blue Pig *(Route 2)*
3. Gauxholme *(Route 3)*
4. Pecket Well *(Route 4)*
5. Stake Lane *(Route 5)*
6. Shibden Dale *(Route 8)*
7. Beacon Hill *(Route 8)*
8. Cock Pit Lane *(Route 9)*
9. Back Lane *(Route 15)*
10. Springfield Lane *(Route 20)*

Appendix

Tourist Information Centres

For tourist information online,
visit: www.yorkshire.com

Batley	T: 01924 423 172
Bradford	T: 01274 753 678
Halifax	T: 01422 368 725
Haworth	T: 01535 642 329
Hebden Bridge	T: 01422 843 831
Holmfirth	T: 01484 222 444
Huddersfield	T: 01484 223 200
Ilkley	T: 01943 602 319
Leeds	T: 0113 2425 242
Todmorden	T: 01706 818 181
Wakefield	T: 01924 305 000
Wetherby	T: 01937 582 151

Weather

www.bbc.co.uk/weather
www.metoffice.gov.uk

Bike Shops

Blazing Saddles – Hebden Bridge
T: 01422 844 435
www.blazingsaddles.co.uk

Ellis Briggs Cycles – Shipley
T: 01274 583 221
www.ellisbriggscycles.co.uk

Aire Valley Cycles – Keighley
T: 01535 610 839
www.airevalleycycles.com

Pedalsport –Halifax
T: 01422 361 460
www.pedalsport.co.uk

Drakes Cycles – Leeds
T: 0113 249 0326
www.drakescycles.co.uk

Accommodation

Youth Hostels

Visit www.yha.org.uk

Haworth	T: 0845 371 9520
Mankinholes	T: 0845 371 9751

Other Accommodation

There are many websites listing places to stay
from bunkhouses to top hotels. Or give the local
Tourist Information Centre a call.

Food and Drink

Cafés

The Bear Café .... T: 07714 333 230
Todmorden

Coffee Cali .... T: 01422 845 629
Hebden Bridge

Pubs

Stubbing Wharf .... T: 01422 844 107
Hebden Bridge

Stansfield Arms .... T: 0113 250 2659
Apperley Bridge

Useful Websites

www.singletrackworld.com – Singletrack Magazine

Other Publications

Yorkshire Dales Mountain Biking – The South Dales. Nick Cotton, Vertebrate Publishing – www.v-publishing.co.uk

Peak District Mountain Biking – Dark Peak Trails. Jon Barton, Vertebrate Publishing www.v-publishing.co.uk

Mountain Biking Trail Centres – The Guide. Tom Fenton, Vertebrate Publishing – www.v-publishing.co.uk

Pennine Bridleway South Map – Derbyshire to South Pennines. Harvey Maps – www.harveymaps.co.uk

About The Author

Benjamin Haworth has been writer for almost ten years, a photographer for fifteen years and a mountain biker for twenty years. He has written countless magazine features and route guides for the UK mountain bike press, most notably for the esteemed and highly regarded Singletrack Mountain Bike Magazine. Although he's a born and bred Lancastrian, he freely admits that West Yorkshire is his favourite place to ride. Rarely a week goes by without Benjamin riding and exploring the South Pennines.

Vertebrate Publishing

Mountain Bike Rider (MBR) Magazine called our MTB guides *"...a series of glossy, highly polished and well researched guidebooks to some of the UK's favourite riding spots."*

We want to provide you - the rider - with well-researched, informative, functional, inspirational and great-looking MTB guidebooks that document the superb riding across the length and breadth of the UK. So if you want to go riding somewhere, you can count on us to point you in the right direction.

As well as our series of MTB guidebooks, we have award-winning and bestselling titles covering a range of leisure activities, including; cycling, rock climbing, hillwalking and others. We are best known for our MTB titles, including the bestseller Dark Peak Mountain Biking, which BIKEmagic.com said was *"far and away the best Peak guide we've come across"*.

Our autobiography of the British rock climbing legend **Jerry Moffatt** won the *Grand Prize* at the *2009 Banff Mountain Book Festival.*

We also produce many leading outdoor titles for other publishers including the Mountain Leader and Walking Group Leader Schemes (MLTUK) and rock climbing guidebooks for the British Mountaineering Council and the Fell and Rock Climbing Club. For more information, please visit our website: www.v-publishing.co.uk or email us: info@v-publishing.co.uk

MOUNTAIN BIKING GUIDEBOOKS

About the Great Outdoors

The great outdoors is not bottom bracket friendly; beautiful flowing singletrack can give way suddenly to scary rock gardens, hard climbs can appear right at the end of a ride and sheep will laugh at your attempts to clean your nemesis descent. Of course it's not all good news. You'll need a good bike to ride many of the routes in our set of mountain biking guides. You'll also need fuel, spare clothing, first aid skills, endurance, power, determination and plenty of nerve.

Bridleways litter our great outdoors. Our guides, written by local riders, reveal the secrets of their local area's best rides from 6 to 300km in length, including ideas for link-ups and night-riding options. Critically acclaimed, our comprehensive series of guides is the country's bestselling and most respected – purpose-built for the modern mountain biker.

The Guidebooks

Each guidebook features up to 28 rides, complete with comprehensive directions, specialist mapping and inspiring photography, all in a pocket-sized, portable format. Written by riders for riders, our guides are designed to maximise ride-ability and are full of useful local area information.

MOUNTAIN BIKING TRAIL CENTRES THE GUIDE

TOM FENTON

Mountain Biking Trail Centres – The Guide
is the only comprehensive guide to the UK's
network of purpose-built, off-road mountain
biking trails, featuring thousands of kilometres of
singletrack, cross country, downhill, freeride and
bike park riding at 67 centres across England,
Scotland and Wales.

Included are classics such as Dalby, Coed y Brenin
and Glentress, lesser-known centres such as Balblair
and Coed Trallwm, together with more recent
developments including Whinlatter, Rossendale
Lee Quarry and many new trails at existing centres.

"*This is without doubt the most comprehensive guide
of its type available.*" MBR Magazine, Guidebook of the Month

"*67 centres across England, Scotland and Wales are covered so if you're
planning some trips, this is a must read before you load the car.*" BIKEmagic.com

"*If you're planning an excursion to any trail centre, this book is a real gem.
And if the pictures throughout the book don't inspire you to ride,
we don't know what will.*" Bikeradar.com

"*An absolute must for every committed trail rider in the country.*" planetFear.com

"*This guide is essential for upping the quality of life of anyone with a
mountain biking gene – just buy it.*" Adventure Travel Magazine

"*If you ride bikes in the UK you simply can't afford to live
without this book.*" Amazon Review

VERTEBRATE PUBLISHING

Available from all good book shops, bike shops
and direct from **www.v-publishing.co.uk**

For the most extreme conditions in the world
www.rab.uk.com